GOD'S GREATEST GIFT OF LOVE

On Mixed Feelings of Hurt and Pain

MARY K. GREEN

authorHOUSE®

AuthorHouse™
1663 Liberty Drive
Bloomington, IN 47403
www.authorhouse.com
Phone: 1-800-839-8640

Published by AuthorHouse   07/21/2012

ISBN: 978-1-4772-4515-6 (sc)
ISBN: 978-1-4772-4514-9 (e)

This book is dedicated to:

My two children who have been wonderful and great children and that I am so proud of.

My daughter, Rolanda Lewis, who has been a great caretaker and like a bridge over troubled waters through the good and bad.

My son, Demetrias Lewis, who has become a great, successful young man as well as loving and trustworthy.

My daughter in law, Kimaree Lewis, who is loving and dedicated.

My seven grandchildren, Zaria, Jamiah, Cincere, Prayher, Primere, Arrion and Rodney(Boss)

My sister and her husband

My brother and his wife

My eleven nephews and nine nieces

My aunts, uncles, and cousins

My church family, at Mt. Calvary #2, who have in so many ways touched my life by being caretakers, prayer warriors, telephone callers, visitors, monetary givers or loving people.

My pastor, Rev. James Lee Smith Sr., who has been a great Spiritual leader and 1st Lady, Drucilla Smith, who has been a joy and loving friend.

In loving memory of:

My mother-Annie Neal Stevenson
My father-Adam Stevenson
My sister-Joann Willard-Vaught
My brother-Amos Stevenson

Contents

Introduction

How do I Deal

    With my Hurt and Pain

This book is being introduced to you by a lady named Kate, who at a young age had some great days and then some difficult days. She will be sharing some sad ones and then some very hurtful days of her life that turned to be very painful. She will also share stories from her childhood to an adult. A young lady who got married and thought she had it all.

As you read her story, you will learn how she had to learn how to deal with many storms, how she survived a long period of suffering within her body, and how her parents brought her up in a church as a young child but when she became a young woman she felt she would not go to church anymore because she wanted to live her life and enjoy the things she thought she was missing. After traveling down that road she had to go back to where she started from because she found out the world meant her no good.

Kate is sharing her story with you in hopes that it will touch someone's heart to help them feel better about themselves. If you are at the turning point in your life that you feel you don't know which way to go, you won't give up, but turn your life around to Christ.

She will let you know that Jesus is the way, he can Heal, Deliver, and Restore, because there is no problem too big for Christ.

He can solve any problem and fix any situation that we may face. She is also praying that whoever may take the time out to purchase one of her books they will be Blessed, have a different look on life after hearing about her life. Giving the most glorious understanding, much encouragement to hold on, no matter what you may be experiencing.

In life, putting in remembrance someone else's situation may be worse than yours. May God Bless All of You!

Chapter 1

There was a little girl named Kate, who was born May 10,1957 in Horry County, South Carolina, her parents lived in Brunswick County, North Carolina at the time when she was born, in a little community called Longwood, where her mother was from. Her father was from a little community called Brooksville. They married and decided to live in her mother's home town.

They lived on a farm in a small three bedroom house. It was red with siding, chickens and dogs all around. One of the chickens (rooster) was very mean. It would peck you when you would step outside. After being married a few years they decided to have children. They ended up having five children, three girls and two boys.

As time progressed, Kate's father started thinking of how he could increase the farming. He had shared farming with a gentleman for many years. Her mother would help out as much as she could, but he knew that soon he would have more help. But as some of you may remember, back in the 50's and 60's that's how people lived. Because they planted and grew most of their food, they did not have to go to the store and purchase a whole lot. During the time of waiting for the crop to grow, Kate's father had a brother and they would sit around and hold mild conversations, his brother told him during one of their conversations, that he could see him having those two boys of his men before he knew it. Her father agreed with him and said "yeah, and those girls too." As they continued talking, her uncle said that he had nicknames for all of the kids.

Her father asked him, what were the names? Her uncle began to laugh. He named one Butterball, because she was short and chubby and had bowed legs, one was Jabo, because he always stayed busy, another was chicken, because she was very small like a bird, then there was Frogman, because when he would sleep, he would get up on his knees like a frog, and finally, there was Tweety Bird, because there had not been another baby for six years after Frogman. Tweety Bird was the cutest little thing, with just one plat sticking up on the top of her head. But of course they had her spoiled.

Kate was not too sure what her daddy meant when he said that the girls would be like the boys, but she found out in a hurry. He planted more and more tobacco, each year he would increase the number of acres, along with sweet potatoes, cotton, watermelons, cantaloupes, butter beans and pole beans. She believed if it could grow, he planted it. Of course she knew it was going to be on her and Jabo at first, because they were the oldest.

Her mother and father were getting ready to walk out of the front door to go to the field to crop tobacco one morning. As her mom was stepping off the porch the chicken (rooster) began pecking her. When it did, she grabbed the chicken by it's neck and would not turn it loose. She rang the chicken's neck off. Kate and the others were in the house laughing. As they were laughing they heard their daddy say, "When me and the kids would tell you the chicken was pecking us", you said, "well any how, the chicken had never pecked you."

her mom replied, that it was the first time it happened and it would be the last. They laughed and laughed.

I'm sure when you read about the nicknames you were wondering which one was Kate. She was Butterball, the little, short, chubby girl that got teased, criticized, and her cheeks would get pulled on all the time because they were so plump. She had long hair. Her mother would put her hair in a ponytail most of the time.

When Kate was in the seventh grade, she would get on the bus and it seems she would always be sitting in front of this girl named Carla. Carla was always picking and teasing her. She would pull her plats (hair) and laugh at her and say very bad things. Kate would go home and tell her parents and would always tell her teacher. As she would talk to them it seemed to her nothing was ever being done. So one day she decided to take matters in her own hands. She was tired of crying and letting the other kids pick at her because Carla would not stop. It seemed as though Carla, did not understand the word "STOP". So one afternoon, it was almost time for the bell to ring to go home. Kate already knew what was going to happen, so she sharpened two pencils, letting the lead get very sharp. She placed the pencils in a pencil bag, where the points would not get broken. As she entered the bus, she, as always, sat in the seat in front of Carla. When she sat down, Carla began pulling her ponytails. Kate did not begin to cry, she reached into her bag and took the pencils out and began to stick Carla. When she did this, Carla put her face in her way and the pencil point went into Carla's eye. It scared Kate so bad. The bus pulled over to the side of the street. The bus driver looked at Carla's eye and said they would have to turn around and go back to the school. All of the kids that were siding with Kate began to complain and told the bus driver that she was only defending herself. The bus driver said, "yes, but Carla's eye is bleeding and Kate couldn't take matters in her own hands." As Kate was listening, she sat very still and quietly. When they returned to the school, the bus driver asked for Kate and Carla to get off the bus. Kate was very scared. When entering inside the school, the school nurse and some of the teachers were still there. The nurse told the bus driver that she would take care of Carla and would find out if Kate's teacher was still there. When the school nurse told Kate to go and see if her teacher was still there, she found Ms. Brown(her teacher) was still there in the class. Ms. Brown asked her why was she there in the class? She told Ms. Brown the story. After Ms. Brown heard what she had done, she told her that she could have put Carla's eye out. Kate tried to explain that she didn't mean to stick her in the eye, but Carla had stuck her face there in the way. Ms. Brown told her that she would have to call her parents. Kate began to cry. Ms. Brown asked her, Why was she crying? Kate told her that she didn't mean to stick her in the eye, but she would ask her not to pull her hair but it seemed as though Carla didn't want to understand the word STOP. Ms. Brown called her parents. Her father told Ms. Brown that he would be right there. As they were sitting and waiting for her father to arrive, Ms. Brown talked to Kate and told her that she could not take matters in her own hands. Kate told her that she understood. Whenever Kate's father got there, the nurse brought Carla to the class. She told them that Carla's eye was ok. Kate was so glad to hear that and she told Carla that she was sorry. Carla promised her, she would never pull her hair again.

Kate's father was standing there and he told them he was apologizing for her behavior. Carla's mother told him it was ok because Carla was wrong, but she was glad her eye was ok. Kate was just smiling; she felt her daddy was understanding. Well, when she got in the car, the smile left her face. Her daddy said, "Kate I am surprised at you." She began trying to explain to her father, who was most of the time very easy. He said, "When I get you home, I am going to beat you." Kate began saying, "Daddy I was only trying to take care of myself. You and mama said, tell the teacher and stop coming home crying!" He told her, "yeah, but you could have put her eye out." Kate began to weep softly. She was very surprised at her daddy because most of the time he talked not whipped. She kept weeping until they reached home. She thought maybe he would have a change of mind. Well, the tables turned for her this time. Her father began telling her mother, where she was standing in the kitchen, canning some vegetables. She asked Kate, "why would you do something so bad?" Kate just looked very sharp at her thinking, why explain. She stood silently. Her daddy said that it was ok because he was going to handle it. Kate promised she would never do anything like that again. Kate would soon be thirteen; she was looking forward to becoming a teenager. This would mean that she would be changing schools soon. She had one more year and she would be going to high school. Little did she know, she would be moving from North Carolina or the little community they lived in. But she overheard her parents talking about buying a home in Brooksville, South Carolina, the little community where her dad was from. She did not want to leave North Carolina because she had been going to school there since kindergarten. Jabo, who was her oldest brother, he was very excited because he was already in high school and the other siblings they were still small. Kate told Jabo that she had already gotten used to those kids picking and saying hurtful things. She felt as though she would have to experience this all over again. Jabo told her, "maybe not." Well, her parents decided to move. On Kate's first day of school, the teacher insulted her. She asked her what her name was. She told her. The teacher wrote her name on the board and as a middle name it was supposed to be Kate, but she wrote CAKE. She began trying to straighten out her name. The class would not stop laughing. But there was one young man who did not think it was funny. The teacher told her that she was sorry, that she had misunderstood her. The bell finally rang for lunch. Kate was so happy. She did not want any lunch. She asked if she may be excused and go outside. The teacher told her yes. As she was sitting at the picnic table she noticed the young man who did not laugh, had walked up and stood beside her. He said to her that he was sorry about the class being rude. She looked at him with a smile and said that it was ok. Her parents had a small home in North Carolina and now that they were growing up, they needed more room. So they decided to move to South Carolina, where her daddy was from. The young man introduced himself, his name was Craig. As Kate was popping her gum they talked and talked. Well the rest of her day was ok. She told Jabo about the young man that she had met. Kate and Jabo were very close. They thought maybe moving, would mean they wouldn't have to farm anymore—that was the wrong answer. Her parents would drive them every evening afterschool and their homework was done to pick cotton, tomatoes, cucumbers, watermelons, sweet potatoes, peanuts, peppers, cantaloupes, collards, and anything that needed to be harvested. If they even thought that it would grow, it would get planted. Kate felt the worst of it all was picking cotton and planting the tobacco. She would tell Jabo by him being a boy, he would have to do work on the farm for a long time, but she hoped that someday someone would marry her and take her away.

Kate was finally getting adjusted to the new school. She started making new friends. It seemed her and Craig were becoming the best of friends. He had become more anxious about talking, doing homework together, and exchanging telephone numbers. Craig and Kate would talk about how soon they would be going to high school. She had made many friends. Still there were a few who would pick & tease her. Her father was noticing that chicken was growing up and getting older so he decided to plant a little more of tobacco. Kate would tell her girlfriends how her father was a farmer. They would all laugh, but she would tell them that they didn't really have to shop at the grocery store. Time was really passing by. Jabo had graduated but he still was helping on the farm, just as Kate had told him. She knew it would soon be her day. Her and Craig had grown very fond of each other but it was very hard for her to date him because her parents were very strict. She finally got the courage to ask them could she have company. They said, "yes" so Craig came over to meet them. Her parents told him he would have to be there by seven and leave by eleven. If they went to the movies, sometimes Kate was ok with the set up but Craig was not. She would have to always remind and tell him that he should be glad of their time that they could be together, because she was surprised they let them see each other. Kate's idea of becoming an RN was not going to happen because Craig wanted to get married and join the military. Every now and then she would talk about it around her mother. Her mother would always tell her, how she should follow her dream. She could see it was making her mother very upset to talk about it so she would not. She always talked to her girlfriends about it. Then one day out of nowhere, Jabo told their father that he was going to get married but he did not want to farm any longer. Chicken's boyfriend had told him also that he was going to marry her also because she was pregnant. So Kate went to the school the next day and she began telling Craig the news. Craig looks at her and said, "well, I was going to ask your parents could I marry you." Kate looked at Craig, and could not believe what she was hearing. But she asked him, what was going to happen with her dream of going to school to become an RN? But he insisted that he wanted her to be with him traveling. She thought back on what she had said to Jabo about someone marrying her and not having to farm. But after everything started happening she thought about her daddy's passion. What was he going to do because he and her mother could not run the farm alone? Kate told Craig to let her think about it before he said anything to her parents.

She was in her last year of school. She thought about Craig leaving and going off into the military, her career, and her mother. What was this going to do to her, because she was very much set on her becoming an RN. Then there was her daddy, who would have no help on the farm, because Frogman and Tweety Bird were really too small. But one thing she knew, she loved Craig and loved her parents and didn't want to hurt neither, because of the dreams they had for her. Craig and Kate would talk every night before going to bed. But she still could not talk to him because he was looking for an answer. So as she laid across her bed, thinking on everything she began piecing everything in her mind. She knew she loved her parents. But she had to give Craig an answer. She thought about her and Craig had been friends since 8th grade, her first love. She laid her head down and got very quiet, when she overheard her mom and dad in the kitchen talking. She could hear her daddy say, that if Jabo and Chicken both were getting married he would have to farm a smaller crop the next year. Her mother had an old saying, "well any how, Kate has been talking about going to nursing school. Her daddy then said, maybe he would just quit the farming and start driving big trucks, transporting furniture to different stores. That right then, at the that moment, gave Kate her answer. She went running out of the room and found Jabo and told him what Craig had told her. Jabo laughed and told her that their father was going to keep her in the field. She told him, no he wasn't because, if he was going to be leaving, so was she.

Jabo said to her, that he was not leaving the area, he just didn't want to farm any longer. Well it was the next day at school, Craig met Kate at the bus stop, he asked her what had happened or why she didn't talk to him the night before. She told him that she had to think. So he asked her if she had an answer. She explained to him that he had to talk to her parents and it might not be very good.

He wanted to know if she loved him, she said "yes," he said that he would take care of everything. He made it sound like it was so easy. He told her that he would be coming over by the weekend. Kate was excited as the days passed, but she was not sure how the visit would be. She was very nervous when Craig came in. After he had spoken to everyone she told him to sit for a little while before he asked to speak to her parents. As they sat and talked she told Craig how they might be very much against it. Craig told her that he loved her and he could not think of the idea of her not traveling with him. So Kate said ok. As she called for her parents she felt they were going to be very upset.

When Craig began talking, he told them he wanted Kate's hand in marriage. Her father just nodded his head and said ok, she could see the disappointment. Her mother said, "well anyhow, I want you to get married," and asked what happened to her going to be an RN? Kate just sat and looked, but Craig told them in the traveling, Kate could pursue her career but Kate knew her mother was upset. Her parents left the room. Kate told Craig she was ok, she had to live her own life. As Craig got up to leave, they asked them when would they be getting married. Craig told them that they had not set a date, but he would be leaving for the Air Force in September. They said ok. Craig and Kate began trying to set a date but everything was moving so fast. They were to graduate May,1975. Jabo was getting married August of 1975 and so was Chicken.

After finally talking with both sets of parents they came up with December, 1975. When the day for Craig to leave came, it was the hardest day for Kate. She told her parents she would be there to help gather the entire crop for the year. They all got together and helped their daddy and he did not farm any longer. She would talk to Craig every day and they were getting so excited that he soon would be home to get married. Their wedding date was December 31, 1975. They got married and their parents gave them a nice reception at Kate's parents' house. They stayed between both parents home for one week. Craig only had a week off. He had to be in Chicago, Illinois by the 2nd week in January.

Kate and Craig said their goodbyes, they began to drive to Chicago. Craig telling Kate everything she had to expect with the military life. It seemed as if it was taking forever to get there, but finally they were at their destination. Everything looked so different. All pretty and white. Snowflakes were still dropping. Craig called and let the officer know they were there, they had to go by the base, they told them they had found them an apartment. It was close to a railroad track and very noisy. Kate began looking at Craig.

When reaching the apartment Craig said to Kate, "I am so sorry but we shouldn't be here long." Everyday when Craig would go to work Kate would sleep late and make sure dinner was ready by the time he would get home. She would be so bored. Finally Craig had one of his friends come by and they all became friends. They joined together to play cards. Kate wanted to get a job but Craig told her it was ok because they would only be there for one and half years.

Many days it was best to stay inside because of so much snow. There were times it was very hard for Craig, with only the one income. Sometimes they would have to eat popcorn but always said they would never call home for anything. They would tell their friends they had to get through the hard times. They loved each other and had each other. They made it through. Craig finally got orders to Austin, Texas. He took some time off to pack everything. Kate was so happy because she wanted to get settled to the next base so she could get a job.

Chapter 2

Craig and Kate are on their way to Austin, Texas. It took them about 4 days of driving. When reaching Texas, they found this was a very big base and Austin was the capital of Texas. So Kate was excited, she knew she could find work. First they checked into a motel. Craig began looking around to find somewhere for them to live. They found a two bedroom apartment downtown, not far from the base. After getting settled Kate began telling Craig how she was going to begin looking in the news paper for a job. He asked, why? She explained that one of the reasons was so she would not be bored in such a large town. He was ok with the idea, but he would rather that she not work. Well as time passed he came and told Kate they were at a base that would be deploying a lot. Kate let him know that she knew then that she really had to find something to do. Craig wanted to know how would she manage getting to & from the job after he have been deployed.

This was a time when she wished she knew how to drive. She had been talking to Craig about this for a while, or since they had gotten married. But he would say why or how he liked taking her everywhere. But she hated him driving her everywhere, because she always felt she had to rush. She told him if she found a job, she had seen where they had bus routes. She was very excited. She began looking for job openings. They had an add in the news paper about needing a laundry supervisor, so she told Craig that she wanted to apply. Craig began telling her that he felt as though that type of job would be too hard and too hot for her. She looked at him and asked, "did you forget I was a farm girl?" he said to her, "you are right," so he took her to apply. Kate was hired, she was so happy because when Craig would be deployed she would not be left at home all day long with nothing to do. Until Craig had to leave he would drop her off at work, it was on the way to the base. Finally Craig was deployed and Kate had to learn the bus route. It was not hard at all. She had met many people that were riding the transit. She needed to find her an assistant manager for the laundry room. She interviewed many people, she finally found someone that qualified for the position. They were able to work together. It seemed as though Craig was getting deployed out very often. But the military women had to gear up because Uncle Sam had a saying, "you may be married, but your spouse is married to Uncle Sam." Kate seemed to be meeting the neighbors, most everyone was friendly. While Craig was gone, Kate began to feel very ill at work one day. She told her assistant that she was leaving work early because she felt as if she had caught a virus. She stayed out of work for 2 days. She called her assistant and told her she was going to the doctor to see what was going on with her. When she got to the doctor's office they began taking vital signs and they couldn't find anything wrong. The nurse began asking questions and about taking a pregnancy test. Kate looked real big eyed and said, she didn't know, but that could be the problem, and that she had just recently gotten married. Everyone in the doctor's office began to giggle. She took the pregnancy test and it came back positive. She became very hysterical about the news. She was so excited, but she knew Craig was not at home to share the good news.

She couldn't call home or tell anyone in the neighborhood, not even on her job. She finally went back to work. When she would get ready for work, she could not eat breakfast because it would make her sick(nauseated) and didn't want her assistant and co-workers to know. Craig would be home in about 3 weeks. One morning her assistant came in with breakfast. Kate was very disturbed, she didn't know what to do because, if she ate the breakfast she knew that she would get sick.

So she kept saying she wasn't hungry and of course her assistant did not want to hear that. So Kate ate, and when she did she became very sick. Her assistant began asking many questions. Kate began to smile, as her assistant asked, "oh my God, are you pregnant?" She looked at her and nodded, "yes." She told her, please don't say anything until she could tell Craig. She said, "ok." That was a relief for Kate, she finally had someone to talk to.

Now it was time for Craig to come home from deployment. Kate was very quiet after picking Craig up from the airport. She wanted to wait unit she could fix him a great dinner before telling him the great news. So when arriving home, she began dinner, talking very slow. Finally dinner was prepared, they sat down to eat, Kate says to Craig, "we are having a baby." Craig looks up from eating, looking very bug eyed. And asked her what did she say. She said, "you are going to be a daddy."

Craig was so happy, he hugged her very tight and then began making phone calls. Calling home first and then walking on the balcony and began yelling to the top of his lungs, "we are having a baby." Everyone was very excited for them. Craig became very persistent and did not want Kate to work anymore, wanting her to get proper rest, etc. Kate told him, that she thanked him for being so loving and caring, but she wanted to continue working as much as possible as long as she could. The pregnancy was very rough for her with all the morning sickness. Craig was still going on deployments. Kate was finally 6 months pregnant, when she felt she couldn't go any longer, so she told her assistant that she would be going on maternity leave.

When going on maternity leave she became very bored so she decided she would start babysitting for one of their neighbors, who could not find anyone to keep her child. As time went by, he was lots of company for her. Craig came home from deployment, seeing how big Kate was, at this time she was eight months pregnant. He went into work and put in for a leave of absence. Kate was so happy. She had her husband to go back and forth to the doctor with her instead of her friend (Jan). The next morning, Craig leaves for work, the base was not very far from where they lived. Every morning before he would leave for work he would tell her to call if she needed him but because she was getting so close to her due date he would come home everyday for lunch. Kate decided to have lunch ready one day. The baby was crying, she had turned the gas oven on, she left the kitchen to console the baby, she rocked the baby and he fell asleep. She put the baby on the bed. When returning, she had forgotten that she had turned the oven on, and being that she was so big from the pregnancy, she kneeled down on her knees to light the oven, fire flames blazed and caught her hair on fire. Back in that day they wore the style of an afro. Kate was very lucky, there was a wet cloth on the kitchen counter. She grabbed the towel and began putting her hair out. She was very scared when getting herself together, she called Craig in a very exciting voice. Craig got her calmed down telling her he would be right there. But as she waited she called her friend from downstairs. Jan came running. As they sat waiting, Kate crying and holding onto the little boy whom she was keeping. Jan kept telling Kate, that it was going to be ok, her hair may have been singed but her face was ok. When Craig got home he took the baby and gave him to Jan, telling her to call his mother because he was going to call the doctor to take Kate to be checked out. Jan said ok. Kate's nurse told Craig to bring her in being she was 8 ½ months pregnant. As Craig and Kate were riding down the highway she seemed to be worried about wearing a wig. Craig told her to not worry because that didn't matter to him, he was just glad it was not worse than it was. Everyone was fine. The nurse got Kate checked in and the doctor came and began examining her. Asking what had happened. The doctor told them, Kate was ok, she was not in labor but he let her know how lucky she was that it did not get her face. As Kate listened to the doctor she told him she was so scared. She had forgot that she had turned the oven on. Kate and Craig left the dr. office saying they had to find a wig shop. When reaching home Jan met them at the car. Jan was Kate's best friend. Craig told Jan, "no she's not in labor."

Kate and Craig lived in a big neighborhood being mostly military. Everyone was mostly close. Kate was getting down to her last few days before her due date. All of a sudden she began craving watermelon and popcorn. It seemed she could not get enough. She was finally in her 9th month. She began having pain in her lower part of her stomach. She was getting very scared. She and Craig had no family there. She would often call home for advice from Craig and her parents. She did not want to go to the emergency room on false pretense. Craig would tell her, not to worry, they would go as many times as they had to, because he didn't want to deliver a baby. So she did just that. Soon she was actually in her 10th month of pregnancy, they became very worried. Kate's mom told her maybe she had miss calculated when she got pregnant. Kate said no, she did not think so, but maybe she had. But Craig told her they had been going back and forth on the base and he was beginning to worry. He was going to take her downtown to another doctor to get a different opinion. Kate was very much in agreement with him, because she was so big and miserable. She made an appointment with another GYN doctor. When they reached the office they got her prepared for the examination, they were so nervous. The nurse said the doctor would be right there. The doctor began to examine her, he says to the nurse, would she help Kate get dressed and he would talk to Craig. Kate could not get dressed fast enough. When the nurse showed her to the room where Craig was, she saw the look on his face, she began to question him. He tells her to sit down, he said to her the doctor had stepped out, that he would be right back. She asked, "what's wrong?" Craig said, "he said that you will have to be hospitalized as soon as possible." Kate knew there had to be something wrong because she had been having very bad pain in the lower part of her stomach. The doctor came back in the room. Kate began asking many questions, he said he could not tell her anything until she was admitted to run test. The doctor told them to go straight over to the hospital. Craig said that he knew something was wrong every time that she had said that she was hurting and he took her to the emergency room. Kate told him to calm down, let her get admitted and they run the test and then they would know. They did, they ran all sorts of test. The doctor finally entered the room and began explaining. One of the tests that they had done showed the baby had a bowel movement inside of her, saying this was not good news, and that they had to remove the baby as soon as possible. Craig became very furious and angry. He began telling the doctor how he had taken Kate back and forth to the doctor on base and they would continue telling them it was not time. She would complain about the pain, Kate began trying to calm Craig down by telling him it was not the time to worry about that. The doctor says now we have to take care of her and the baby as soon as possible. Craig agreed, he told the doctor he was just scared for the two of them. The doctor said he understood but they would be doing all they could do. Craig asked, what could he do to help.

The doctor said to just hold her hand. Kate looked at him and said, "Pray." As she laid there she was very quiet, waiting for the doctor to return back in the room. Craig told Kate he was going to call home and let everyone know, so they could Pray. The nurse began telling Kate that they needed to check and see how far the baby had dropped. When doing the test, it showed the baby had not dropped at all because her pelvic bones were built too close.

The doctor came back into the room saying, with the baby having a bowel movement and Kate's pelvic bones so close their maybe complications but they would give her a spinal tap. She would be awake through the entire procedure because putting her to sleep would not be good because what they may run into when starting the delivery. He told Craig if the baby had dropped, Kate may not have made it. So they would be trying very hard not to induce labor, they would be performing a C-section. Kate told Craig if there were any decisions to be made during the procedure she knew that he would make the right decision. The anesthesia doctor came in and gave her an epidural. Soon her body was numb, she was able to talk to Craig and nurse's as they began cutting. Well it was not long they were looking at a beautiful 9 pound, 8 ounce little girl. As the doctor passed the baby over to the nurses, they realized the baby was not crying and she was turning blue. The doctor grabbed the baby back and began spanking the baby's bottom. The baby began crying, they rushed out of the room with the baby in their arms leaving Kate and Craig devastated with so many questions. The nurse told Craig at that moment, they had to concentrate on getting Kate sewn back up, cleaned up, and transfer her to a different bed. Kate was crying very softly, and asking, "can someone please tell us about our baby?" The nurse said very low, "we just don't know. Of course when we know, we will let you know." Kate did not want to hear that. Craig began walking and pacing the floor, he said he felt so helpless, he could not do anything. The pediatrician doctor came in, Kate was laying downward position but she sat straight up. Craig stood still right where he was. The doctor began to talk, he said the baby had meningitis. Kate asked, "can you explain what that is?" as she is crying. Craig walked over holding her hand. She said to the doctor; "please don't tell us our baby will die." He says they would be doing all they could. The baby had been in the water for 10 months and by having the bowel movement inside of her that it had caused an infection. With this infection of the membranes, which deals with the brain and spinal cord could become very fatal. But as you pray, we will be starting a very mild antibiotic for the baby, keeping a very close watch. Kate and Craig knew this was not good news, but told the doctor they believe they would do all they could do. As Kate was telling the doctor "thank you," she broke down and began to cry. Telling Craig would he please call her mother. When hearing her mother's voice she began to cry that much louder and harder. Her mother said to her, "we are Praying, you have to trust God." She said she wished that she could be there. She told her mother she had not been Praying but she knew that was the only thing that could be done. The nurse came in and said the doctor will be releasing the baby and she would be bringing the baby to the room. She wanted to know what her name was going to be. Craig jumped up and said that's my little girl. He was going to name her. Kate looked at the nurse and said, "well as you can see I have no say so." The nurse laughed. Craig gave her the name. Kate was shocked because they had only been discussing boy names, because he was so sure it was a boy. Craig told her, that he was sorry he was ready for a boy or girl. So the nurse wrote the name down when she came with Patrice (her middle name) they had shaved her hair off on both sides of her head. Having tubes being run from each side, tubes in her little arms and a small heart monitor, could not believe they could make something so small. Kate and Craig could only look at her with tears running down their face. The nurse said she would be back in about an hour to get Patrice. It seemed the hour went by so fast. The nurse was back, as the nurse reached for Patrice, Craig looked at the nurse and said, "that's my little girl, she's got to make it." The nurse nodded her head saying, "yes." Kate was progressing from the surgery good. The doctor was glad. He told her after a few days she could go home. Many of their friends and co-workers would come by the hospital to see her and the baby. But because Patrice had the infection they could only look at her through the window. Craig and Kate knew this was best. It was time for Kate to go home, she was excited but her excitement went away when the pediatrician doctor came in and said Patrice was doing great but they felt they needed to keep here for another week. Kate then did not want to go home. The next day she asked her doctor could she stay another week. The doctor said normally they don't let the patient stay, but because she didn't drive they would do it this time. Kate was happy. Craig said he was relieved because he knew she would want to be with Patrice. As days went by Patrice began to get stronger. The prayers were working, they started removing the tubes and the monitor. It was a blessing to see that Patrice was going to live. At the end of the week Kate could call Craig for them to go home. Craig went on leave from work, it was great having him around, but his leave was short. They had to go on deployment. They were very upset. Kate asked Craig, what was she going to do? He told her to call home. When calling home their parents suggested that her and Patrice come home. She had not been home since she got married. Since Craig had been going on so many deployments she told them she would be calling back to let them know. When getting off the phone, Kate began asking Craig how could she go home because their was not enough time for him to drive them home. He looked at her and said, "you can fly." She looked at him and asked, "are you crazy?" he says, "no!" She said no because she had never flown before. Craig kept talking to her until she finally said yes. Until she realized she had not talked to the doctor about taking a trip. She told Craig she would call the next day. She was hoping the doctor would say no and he did. She did not want to fly without Craig. Craig said to her the next day, after a long day at work, that he would be going on deployment for 2 months. Kate felt very sick, she knew then that she needed to take the trip. She told Craig the doctor said that they could not travel for 2 weeks. Craig told her that he would get the ticket and have the money available. Kate did not want him to know how scared she was. She went into the bedroom and called her best friend. Jan told her, "girl its like a piece of cake and don't worry you will enjoy the flight." Craig asked Kate, "if you can't go until 2 weeks, how will you get to the airport?" She said that she would get Jan to take her. She tried to be as brave as possible when talking to him about the situation. Craig sitting at the table always thinking says to Kate, "let's have a get together." This is a random thing that military families did and Kate and Craig had not did one since they had been in Texas. Kate said she was ok with it if it was not going to be a problem because of Patrice. She was not one of those people to drink or party but she would stand by her man. So they began making plans, Craig began calling neighbors who he wanted to come. When Kate called Jan, she asked Kate, why was she going home? She told her that their parents wanted her to come home because Craig would be gone for 2 months on deployment. And they would help her take care of the baby. Jan told Kate, "I understand, but you know my husband will be gone too and I will help you." Kate said, "I know, but you know they want to see the baby." Yes, I forgot its the first grand. Kate said she wanted to go, but since she had to fly she wish Craig would be able to go. Oh well let's not talk about it right now. They began talking about the get together. Of course Jan was the partying type. She would always tell Kate how grown up she was. Time was approaching for everyone to get together, Craig was a great cook. They fixed different hors d'oeuvres. The table was looking great. Kate was getting Patrice ready for bed. After doing so Jan and her husband were the first to come over. Soon the door bell was steady ringing. Kate told everyone that Craig would be out soon. Kate kept smelling baby oil and the scent kept getting stronger and stronger. She didn't understand why. Craig finally came out of the bathroom and when Kate looked up and saw his hair she was very puzzled. He had his hair split on the side and it was laying down from brushing with baby oil. The guys began saying, "man what's going on with your hair?" Kate just standing looking very widely waiting for his answer. Craig said, "man I got good hair when I take time to groom it, Patrice has hair like me." The guys are drinking and laughing saying, "man we have never seen your hair look like that." Patrice, when she was born had silk black hair, beautiful, but she knew she did not get it from her daddy. But she was not going to embarrass him, so she went along with the conversation. The guys were over in a huddle drinking, playing cards and having a good time. The women they were on the other side of the room. Kate began to hear laughter getting louder and louder. Jan's husband came over and said, "girl, go get your husband." Kate figured he was drunk and had passed out. She jumped up went to the huddle to find that Craig's hair was changing. The baby oil was drying so his hair was just rolling in small balls and flaking up real bad. Kate said to Craig, "oh my God, you need to go to the bathroom." He asked, why? Kate said, "it's your hair." He took off real fast. Kate looked at Bob and told him, "you were wrong for that, you could have told him. "Bob just laughed. When Craig came from the bathroom everyone was laughing. One of his other coworkers wanted to know what happened. By now the only thing he could do was to tell them that he had lied. Well the party was over. Everyone said they had a good time. Two days later, it was time for the guys to deploy. Everyone met in the meeting place. The guys were still talking about the get together. Kate was holding Patrice, one of the guys pulled the blanket back from covering Patrice head, saying, "Craig, now this is what you call silk smooth hair and I believe it looks, like she get it from her mama." Craig said, "ok, you got me on that one." Everyone laughed. It was time for the guys to say good-bye. All the women crying and some men. Craig told Kate he loved her and to take care of his little girl.

When he walked away Jan walked over to Kate and hugged her and said, "we will make it." Kate said, when Craig would leave before it was just me but now I have a baby. Jan said, I know but I will help you until you leave for Myrtle Beach. Kate told Jan she was so glad to have a friend like her. Her and Bob were good people. Kate had to make an appointment for her and Patrice to see the doctor before they left. When seeing the doctors they told her she could travel at any time. She was glad to hear that. When getting back in Jan's car she told her. Jan asked, so when would she be leaving? She said maybe in 2 or 3 days. Jan said ok, but she would miss her. Kate said, her too. She asked Jan, "you know what I want to do when I come back?" Jan asked what? She told her, "I want you to teach me how to drive." She says, "girl you know I don't mind taking you around." Kate said I am very appreciative even when Craig drives me, but it's just that sometime I want to go to the mall or grocery store alone because when he goes with me I feel I have to rush. He always say I don't have to, but you know I be feeling different and now that we have Patrice I need to learn how to drive. Jan said then ok, when you get back that will be a project we will be working on. Jan then told Kate she would be over the next day to help her pack for her trip. She said ok. The next day Kate and Jan done just that. Trying to make sure she didn't forget anything. Kate said to Jan there is so much more to pack, especially now with a baby. Kate called home and told Craig's mother and her mother when she would be leaving. Her mother told her that her father would be picking them up from the airport. Kate would dare not to tell them how scared she was to fly. She was so excited knowing she was going home to see everyone. She gave her mother the time she would be arriving in Myrtle Beach. The next day she would be boarding a plane wishing Craig would be with her. Jan came up stairs and helped her get everything in the car. She told Jan that she was glad that Craig had got the ticket before he left. She said that her stomach felt like it was going to break loose at anytime. Jan said to her, "its just your nerves." When arriving at the airport, Kate was very quiet. She said maybe she should call home and tell them she was not coming. Jan told her girl it's going to be like a piece of cake. They removed all the bags. Telling the desk clerk she wanted to keep several bags on the plane. After getting checked in, it was getting to the time for Kate to board the plane. Her and Jan said their good byes holding Patrice in the carrier. Jan says to her, call me when you get to Myrtle Beach. Kate said ok. Kate is now on the plane, she is looking for her seat, her seat was in the middle she was so glad. There was a lady next to the window and then a nice looking gentleman came and sat on the outside seat. Kate speaks to both of them. The stewardess is walking around telling her to take Patrice out of the carrier and fasten her in the seat belt with her. The gentleman got up and put the carrier away for Kate. She said thanks. She tells him she had never had flown before, and they seemed to strike a very good conversation. The lady was not saying much. Soon Kate was lost for words, as she could feel the plane moving. The gentleman began to laugh, but Kate didn't even look his way. The stewardess began talking about the lights off the exit, the life jackets, how many minutes they would be in the air, and the snack bar would be coming around. They were on a 747, a very nice plane, but she did not feel comfortable. She felt so nervous, she was trying to be cool and calm. The gentleman said to her, "if you get too scared you can hold on to my arm." Kate looks at him and say with great confidence, "I prayed!, I will be ok." He said to her, "ok." Soon the plane began to move faster on the run way. Before Kate knew it she had grabbed the gentleman's arm. He said its ok we will be in the air in just a minute. As Kate looked over at the lady, she was laughing, as she said to her, that is a normal reaction for a person first time flying. The stewardess was now coming around with the snack bar. On this snack bar she saw juices, cokes, peanuts, coffee and alcoholic beverages. In her mind she wanted to tell the stewardess she needed a drink (alcohol beverage) but she didn't even know what kind. So she thought in her mind she better stick to coke or juice. Kate asked the gentleman, "are we in the air?" He told her "yes, we will soon be in Atlanta." Kate says this is not bad. She became very relaxed looking at T.V. and then suddenly there was a big bump, she grabs the man's arm again. They are laughing. He said we are on the run way, they had landed in Atlanta. Kate was so amazed at how big the airport was. The gentleman helped her get off the plane and walked her to the gate and desk. She had to go to Myrtle Beach. He was going to Charlotte. They would be going out of the same gate. Kate was telling him after sitting and waiting how she was so glad her husband had got her ticket for her. Not even 10 minutes of her saying this, they called over the airport intercom, "everyone that is going to Myrtle Beach needs to come to the desk." Kate gets up with Patrice and the young lady told her she needed to see her ticket. When looking at her ticket she said she would have to go and have the ticket changed. Kate was so upset because the airport was so big. The gentleman that sat next to her on the plane asked her what was the problem. She told him, then he suggested to her that his flight was delayed and he would keep Patrice. Kate said, "no thank you, I don't know you." He replied, "but this airport is so big, I don't know where to go, and you have to do so much walking." He also said to her with his pretty blue eyes, "I will be right here, I wouldn't move, you can trust me, I promise." Kate not thinking any longer told the gentleman ok. When walking away Kate told him, "please take care of my baby." She kept looking back and waving until she could not see him any longer. She was so scared, walking as fast as she could, and wishing that Craig was there. When noticing, she was on the other side of the airport. Asking questions and finding out if she was where she was to be to get the ticket changed. Moving as fast as she could to get back to Patrice. Kate remembered the letter over the port she had to go back to. But the airport was so busy. The closer she got to the area she saw no one. She began to get confused and cry because she thought maybe she was lost. She went on up to the desk. But when reaching the desk, she noticed it was not the same girl who had told her that she had to change her ticket. But she went on up to the desk to see if this was the gate to board to go to Myrtle Beach. When she took the ticket out and asked the young lady, she said yes. Kate dropped the ticket and began yelling to the top of her lungs. "My baby!, my baby!," she got lots of attention. They were trying to calm her down to ask what baby. Kate was hysterical, crazy, you name it. The young lady was explaining to some of the people that she did not see a baby. Kate kept yelling. Then the lady that was on the desk when Kate and the gentleman got off the plane walked up, she had been on break. She walked up seeing and hearing all the commotion asking, what happened? She saw that it was Kate. As soon as Kate recognized it was the desk attendant that was originally on duty, she jumped up and asked her if she remembered seeing her with her baby and leaving her with the gentleman that was sitting there? She said, "yes," but his flight had left early. Kate did not give her time to say anything else she just began yelling and yelling. The girl was trying to calm her down but

Kate did not want to listen. So the young lady knew that she was very upset, she was not listening. She walked away and when Kate saw her again she had Patrice. Kate took Patrice and held her so tight. The young lady told her, the gentleman said to tell you that he was sorry he could not wait, his flight was leaving early so he asked her if she could watch her baby and could she give the baby to her. And when it was time for her to go on break she took the baby to the back and left her with one of the other stewardess. She was apologizing for not being back from break and not telling the desk clerk who was covering the desk for her while she was on break. Kate looked at the young lady, grabbed her neck not wanting to turn loose, saying she was sorry she was not listening. The young lady said that it was ok and that she would have reacted the same way. Kate holding Patrice very close. They finally said the flight to Myrtle Beach would be leaving in 30 minutes. Kate was very quiet saying in her mind she never was going to let go of her baby again. When boarding the plane this time she was sitting in the middle of course, but this time there were two men on each side. Kate never talked, only speaking and holding Patrice for dear life. She was not even afraid of flying anymore or it was because when the plane took off and landed she was holding on to Patrice. It was the first experience she had ever experienced and she wanted it to be her last. She knew she did not want her parents or Craig to find out how embarrassed and stupid she was to make such a foolish judgment in trusting someone she didn't even know. She was thankful things went the way that it did because if the gentleman had took Patrice, she could not have lived it down. Because she was already a miracle baby. And she was thinking how she could tell Craig what a foolish judgment she had made. Tears running down her face now, she was seeing her daddy and uncle. So glad to see them. Her daddy asked what was wrong? She just spoke very quickly saying that she missed Craig. They laughed and said, "well you are home now." While waiting for her luggage, Kate cleared her face up. As they approached the car she was getting very excited because she knew her mother was home cooking a great southern meal. And she was very ready for that. When reaching her parents' home that was where her mother sat, in the kitchen. Tweety Bird and Frogman had grew up. It was a great home coming. Jabo and his family lived next door and Chicken and her family lived maybe 5 minutes away. They all came over for dinner. Kate at this time was not able to hold Patrice, from so many hands holding her. So she was missing for a few minutes. Frogman went looking for her and he overheard her talking to Jan about the scene that happened in Atlanta. Kate told Jan she had to get off the phone because she knew she was in trouble. And yes, when she went back in the living room everyone was looking at her with spaced out looks. Her mom asked, "What happened in Atlanta?" She just looked at first saying nothing. Then she began telling them the story. After she finished, everyone of course went crazy saying all sorts of things no matter how bad she already felt. When Kate looked, her father was taking his belt loose and grabbed her by the arm. Everyone was laughing. She looked up at him, pulling away, saying, "daddy what are you doing?" He said, "I am going to beat your ass, because I know you have lost your mind." Kate began to laugh, as she said, "I'm grown." He said, "I know that's why I am going to beat you, because you should have known not to have made a decision so stupid." Kate said, "I know, I just thank God it was not one I had to regret the rest of my life." She said she would never do anything like that again. The time went by real fast. It was always a lot of fun when everyone would get together. It was a great reunion but her time was winding up. Chicken told her they were going to the mall. Kate said ok. The next day when reaching the mall Chicken told her they would be looking for a harness. Kate was like, "why?" She said so you can hold Patrice at all times. So they found one. When getting ready to go back to Texas, Kate and Tweet Bird packed. She told Tweety Bird she was sad because she was going to miss everyone but was glad she would be able to see Craig soon. Kate's daddy was taking her back to the airport. Kate had Patrice in the harness in front of her. Her father said, "I thought you were supposed to put the baby on your back". Kate laughs. She says, "daddy I think it's best I keep her in front of me so I can see her at all times." They were now at the airport, her uncle and father gathered her bags and she checked in. Then it was time for them to say their good byes. Kate began to get teary eyed whenever it was time for them to board the plane, she told them that she would call, when she arrived back to Texas, and she promised that she would hold onto Patrice. They laughed and she got on the plane. As the plane was taking off she was thinking in her mind that there was no problems in Atlanta and when landing there was no problems. She was so happy. The next stop would be in Texas. Kate had called Jan before leaving her parents. She was going to be waiting for her and Patrice. They were glad to see each other. Jan told her she wanted to hear all about her visit. Jan told Kate that she really missed her, with Bob being gone. Kate said just think, it wouldn't be but a few days and the guys would be home. She told Jan she didn't want to tell Craig what happened in Atlanta. Jan said no, let that be a secret for a while and maybe tell him when the time is right. They laughed and said yes. Well Kate was back home. She and Jan unloaded the car. Jan spent the night and they talked and talked. The guys were coming home. Kate wanted to cook something good. When Craig got home they were so glad to see each other. And of course, the first question he asked was, "where is my little girl?" As time went on, Jan did what she had promised. In the afternoon's she started taking Kate to do some driving. Craig said he was upset because she wanted to drive. She was trying to explain to him how she would feel so bad for him waiting and when she went back to work she didn't want to be riding the bus. Craig seemed like he was not happy with the idea but Kate ignored him because this would help her to become more independent. She was glad to go back to work. Everyone was glad to see her and she was glad to see them.

Craig came home from work after a long day and said, to her, "well I got orders again." Kate held her breath and asked, "where?" And he said, Ft. Walton Beach, Florida. Kate told Craig that the was one of the things she didn't like, was making friends and then having to separate. Craig said, he didn't know when they would be leaving, but it is not like they were leaving instantly. But that would be the next base where he would be stationed. Kate could not wait to talk to Jan to see if Bob knew where they would be going. She told her, yes, they would be going to Chicago. Craig and Kate had just came from there. Well Jan and Kate enjoyed every day, even Craig and Bob, before they were going to be deployed.

Kate learned how to drink. Kate had a birthday and Craig allowed her and Jan to go out. Kate was nervous, she didn't do anything wild and crazy but Jan said she was going to expose her to some fun. Kate said, "I don't know girl." "Jan said nothing bad girl," laughing as hard as she could. So she said ok, got dressed for the night out. When Jan and Bob came over for Jan and Kate to leave and Bob staying with Craig. He said to Kate, "don't come home drunk." She told him that he knows she doesn't drink. She didn't know Jan had different plans. She said they were going to a house party but they will be stopping to the store to get some wine. She went in and got 4 bottles of Thunderbird, telling Kate that two of them was for her. They began drinking the wine. Kate thinking it would not make her drunk, they sat in the car laughing and talking never making it to the house party. Kate started to feel sick. She told Jan they had to go home. Jan said, "girl you are not supposed to be drunk off wine." Kate was slurring, her speech, "just take me home, I feel sick." When reaching Kate's home they had to make it upstairs. Jan was laughing but Kate was far from laughing, she felt sick as a dog. When reaching the top of the stairs, Jan knocked on the door, Craig came to the door. Jan was holding Kate up. Craig all as loud as ever, "I know you are not drunk." Kate just went as fast as she could saying nothing, running to the bathroom throwing up everywhere, hearing Craig, Jan and Bob laughing. Craig telling Jan that she knew Kate didn't drink. They left and Craig, came in the bathroom and helped Kate get off the floor. She was on her knees over the toilet, saying, " I'm sorry and I won't drink again." The next day was very rough for Kate at work. She had 2 bad headaches, she could not wait for time to go home. When reaching home, Craig and Patrice, weren't home. Craig would pick her up from daycare. So Kate just crawled in bed. Jan called her when she got home. Kate began telling her that she would not follow her up anymore because she felt terrible. Jan laughs and told her that she just have to get used to it. And that when she does it again it would not be as bad. After Craig and Patrice got home, he put Patrice down in her play pin and went into the bedroom where Kate was in bed and asked, "why are you in bed?" When she told him the reason that she was in bed, he became very angry. Kate asking, "what is wrong?" He replied, "I don't like this at all." Kate wanted to know, what did he mean by saying that? He said, that he used to like Jan, but it looks like she was going to be a bad influence to her. And that she had taught her how to drink. And also she had learned her how to drive. If he had a problem with taking her around, she would have known it. Now it looked as though she would be driving herself everywhere. Kate looked at him with tears in her eyes and asked, "do you think you are to control me? Jan taught me how to drive, because I asked her. When asking you to teach me how to drive, you would always tell me that you would some day. But when I looked at the fact, I was feeling so bad, that you would have to wait for me, if you did not go in the store with me. And the drinking, it was my birthday I tried it and I didn't like it. But you make it sound as if I drink every day. Let me remind you, that you drink, play cards, and smoke the bad stuff with your boys as you can say. Now that it seems I am having a little fun, you are jealous." Craig says to her, "no, he was not jealous." He was used to her being home. Kate told him that most of the time she is still at home, because of Patrice. So please for him not to start having a problem with her because she wanted to go out sometimes. Jan was her only close friend. Well as time went by Kate and Jan would go out from time to time but Craig did not like it. She was still drinking, but not getting drunk. Especially when the guys would get deployed and some of the girls would get together. Kate was not bored anymore. She felt she was fitting in. Craig told Jan, that she was the cause of his wife drinking alcohol beverages. Jan laughed and said, "not a big drinker." He also told her that he couldn't wait for them to leave and that he was glad that Bob's orders were to Chicago. Kate overheard the conversation; she told Craig, "you are wrong!" "Jan did not hold the bottles to my head. I wanted to try it." Since it seems I am letting my hair down it seems you cannot deal with it." She noticed they were beginning to quarrel a lot. More than ever. So Jan and Kate slowed down from going out as much. Of course, doing that Craig was so happy. Then one night prior to them leaving they had Bob and Jan over for dinner. After dinner Craig said to Bob and Jan, let's show Kate how to play cards (spades). Jan laughs and asked, "girl you don't know how to play spades?" Kate said, "no," because she came from a religious home and you better not get caught with a deck of cards in your hand. Everyone was laughing. It was only the four of them. After having too much to drink, Jan yells out, "Kate, did you ever tell Craig about your trip to Myrtle Beach?" By now, Kate is looking very wide eyed. She asked Jan, "what are you talking about girl?" "You are drunk." She then yells out, "what happened in Atlanta?" Kate knew it was not a good time to talk about what happened, because Craig had been drinking also and he had been a butt hole lately. Kate is furious at Jan after she told the story. Kate was just sitting there speechless, feeling very betrayed. Craig started yelling to the top of his lungs, calling her every bad name that anyone could ever call a person. She was so embarrassed, Jan knew she had messed up. She told Bob they should leave. After they left, Craig looks at Kate and asked why didn't she tell him? Kate said she wanted to find the right time. After time went by she didn't think about it. She then broke down and began to cry. She told Craig she knew she should have told him but it scared her so bad she felt he would be upset, and he should be. She never knew he would act the way he did in front of Jan and Bob. She told Craig he was changing. He told her he was sorry but he felt he had lost the woman that he had known since 8th grade. Kate felt that he was so unfair. All she was doing was trying to fit in with the crowd of people they hung around. Craig said a few more words that made Kate tell him she just wanted to go to bed, as she didn't want to hear anymore about the situation. The next day when Jan and Kate saw each other, Kate told her, she never thought she would betray her like that. Jan said she was sorry and she didn't mean to tell. Kate told her Craig had been acting very funny about their friendship since they became close. He had this little ego about himself. Women do what a man say, not what they want to do. So, he has been mad about her for teaching her how to drive and going out. So when she did what she had done the night before, he felt that she could tell her about situations that occur and not him and she knew that it was not like that. Kate knew that she was ready for their orders to come through now because her and Jan's friendship would not be the same. They had been in Texas for three and half years. Their orders came through and Jan and Bob would be leaving for Chicago in 30 days. Their last few days in Texas was not like it used to be but they got through it. Kate could see Craig was glad they were not as close, but she was thinking Craig was not being fair. But she would not bring it up. The time was approaching for them to leave and say their good byes. Jan and Kate held on to each other very tight and Kate told Jan she was forgiven. Jan said she was so relieved, Kate told her she was not looking forward to the ride to Ft. Walton Beach, Florida. Then Craig yelled out and said, "at least we are in the car, we can hold on to Patrice." Kate said, "yeah, yeah, but what about the long ride?" It will take them about three and half days to get there. Craig laughs and says it would be a nice trip because they would be stopping and spending the night in a motel. And then she said, maybe so but think about Patrice and how will she like the trip.

Chapter 3

It was very hot in Texas but very beautiful with a big population and lots of homes. While riding, Craig and Kate talked and when she would bring up Jan's name Craig would try to change the subject. Kate asked him why, and he said that he just didn't care for her. So Kate said, "what if I say I didn't like some of your friends you had coming over?" He said there's nothing that she could say because he was the man and a woman has to stay in a woman's place. Kate just looked at him saying to herself that she was not going to let him hold her back from enjoying life. Patrice was 3 ½ years old and she said she was not going to try to have another baby for 5 years. She would look for her a job, meet some friends to go out with and have a great time. As they rode and stopped, Craig knew Kate was upset with him. He asked her if he had said something wrong. She looks at him and tells him, "yes." And that it seemed as if he was trying to be very controlling. He told her "no, he was not trying to be controlling." Finally, they had reached Ft. Walton Beach, FL. When arriving on the base they were holding a house for them. They had to check into a motel until they got the furniture and things delivered. After a couple of days they were able to move in their new home. When they were settled Craig had to go back to work. Kate was glad, she was ready for a break. As Craig was getting ready to get in the car, Kate and Patrice were standing in the doorway. A lady came from across the street to introduce herself. Craig was backing out but Kate could see his face. He was not going to like that. But she was glad to meet someone. The lady and her husband were from New Orleans. Craig came home for lunch. Kate knew he would have many questions. She told him that they had only talked for a few minutes, and had told her where they were from. Craig asked if she thought they might become friends. She told him probably, and that she seem to be a very sweet girl. Kate asked Craig to please not get there and think he was going to control her life. She couldn't understand why he have changed and seem to have a very jealous feeling about her because she had never given him any reason to. Craig just looked at her. Kate said nothing else to him because she knew she had hit a nerve. He had been acting very stubborn. She was so amazed of his actions but loved him. After being there for a year and half, Kate could not find a job so she decided to go ahead and have another baby. Craig was so excited to hear that. She went to the doctor to get a checkup and the doctor told her that he would be taking her birth control pills. He told her since she had been on birth control for 4 ½ years it may take them a little while before she would get pregnant. Craig was not ok with that. He wanted to go ahead and try. Well, there was another doctor on a base that didn't know what he was talking about. Kate was sick as she could be; she was throwing up like crazy. Craig had taken her to the doctor on the base. He told them that there was no way Kate could be pregnant, that he had examined her and that she had gall stones. Kate looked at the doctor and asked, "are you sure?" He told her that the pregnancy test had came back negative and whenever they did the ultrasound, the results showed that she had gall stones. Craig and Kate left not satisfied. Craig told her, because all of the throwing up, and constant nausea that it was just like when she found out that she was pregnant with Patrice. Kate said, "I know." Craig said he was going to take a day off and take her downtown to be checked by another doctor. Well he did just that. Kate had talked to Pam, her neighbor across the street about a GYN doctor which was her doctor. She began telling the story about the base GYN and that she didn't agree with their diagnosis either. Kate was so glad they were going downtown. When Craig took her to the GYN doctor, the nurse told her to undress, and Kate told the doctor whenever he came in, that they had been on base and he said that she had gall stones. The doctor said ok. Soon as he checked Kate he looked at Craig and started laughing. He told Craig that she was 2 ½ months pregnant. Kate said, "oh my God!, what is wrong with these doctors on the base?"

Craig and Kate told the doctor they would be keeping him for her doctor. And that they would not be going to the base. She didn't want to experience nothing like she did with Patrice. Kate's pregnancy went great. Craig was not going on deployment at this base. It seemed their relationship was doing much better. It was time for her to have the baby. She had a big 10 pound, 14 ounce beautiful boy. Craig was so happy. Kate thought she was going to be able to name the boy. "Wrong answer" . . . he had already told the nurses the name. She had a C-section; she was ok with Craig naming him because everything had gone good. Craig named his middle name Nikeel. When they brought Nikeel to the room one of the nurses had been downstairs and bought a football suit. The suit was so cute. Nikeel was so big he had the suit filled out. He looked just like Craig. Kate thought Craig had such a big smile after Patrice was born, he was worse with Nikeel. He was calling the family, coworkers, buying cigars, giving them out in the hospital and saying, "I got a boy!" Pam, the neighbor, and friend had Patrice, as she was now 5 years old. Kate called her and told her she had a little brother. Patrice told her, "mama, you can come home but the baby can't." Kate asked her why did she say that. She said, because, "if you bring the baby home I will put him in the trash." Kate said, "that's not nice, that's your brother." Whenever Kate got off the phone she told Craig. He laughed. She said, "you laugh, she might just do that." Craig had her so spoiled. Pam brought her up to the hospital. She was moving very slow looking at the baby. When she did, she just looked. Kate knew what she would have to do when she got home. She would let Patrice help with the baby. Finally she got the ok to go home. Craig and Patrice were happy. Pam came over and helped. Craig came home from work looking like he was so tired. He sat down on the chair and Kate asked him what was wrong, he said he got orders to Japan. Kate was surprised to hear that since she had just had a baby and he was only 2 weeks old. Kate asked in a joking voice, "when do you leave" and he said, "in about 2 weeks." She couldn't believe this was really happening. Craig said you got to remember, "I'm married to Uncle Sam." Kate asked how long would he be gone. He told her that he would be gone for a year. She knew in the back of her mind she really was glad for the first time to hear Craig say he had to go away. She felt ok about it. Because maybe they needed a break from each other. But she would never say that to him. She acted as normal. Craig did not want to go because Nikeel would be a month old when he left but he had to go. Kate did not know a lot of people because she was not working, which Craig said he was glad of that. They only had been in Florida a little over a year. Kate knew Pam and her husband and Craig had brought one of his best friends from work to meet her. His name was Will. Whenever he came over, Kate had no idea he was stationed there with them. They got to know him back in Austin. Craig told him to take care of his family while he was gone; and also Pam and Roy to look out for his family. When it was time for Craig to go, Craig got Will to drive Kate and the kids to see him off because the airport was about 1 ½ hours away from the base. Patrice jumped up and down crying because she did not want her daddy to leave. Nikeel was still small and too young, he didn't know what was going on. Kate told Craig to take care of himself, holding on and crying and him saying the same thing and that they loved each other. When turning her a loose he looks at Will again and say, "man I want you to take care of my family and if Kate needs anything, make sure you get it for her." If anything happens that she needs to talk to someone on the base you will be able to help her. Now Kate is thinking in her mind, why would he tell another man to take care of his family, knowing how jealous he had been lately. Craig walked away. They are waving as he entered the plane. They kept waving until they could no longer see each other. As Kate was standing at the window with Nikeel in the harness and Patrice by the hand, she began thinking about what had happened in Atlanta, so she asked Will to pick up Patrice because it was getting very crowded in the airport. Patrice says to Kate, "why mama, I can walk." Kate said, "I know but it is a long story and smiled." When getting back to the car, Kate went to the back to put the kids in their car seats. She noticed Will was standing outside at her car door. When she walked over he opened the door for her. She was thinking, what a gentleman. Craig had been very sweet, but lately things were not the best. She didn't understand what may have happened. The ride back was very quiet, every now and then they would say a word or two. Kate was very happy that Will had drove, because traffic was very bad. But boy was Kate glad she had her license with Craig being gone. When returning back to the base and Kate's home, Will helped get Patrice and Nikeel in the house. He left his number saying if she needed him to call. She said ok, and then after he left she called Pam over to talk. Pam came over, Kate had laid Nikeel on the bed, in the middle of the bed and Patrice was in her room playing. Kate and Pam were in the kitchen, because she had to make Nikeel some bottles. Kate could see Nikeel from the kitchen down the hall. He was just playing so her and Pam was talking away. Kate was telling her how Craig had left Will in charge of his family. Pam began to holler(laugh), "you got to be kidding, that fine man?" Kate agreed with her that he was fine and told her that he had even opened the door for her to get into & out of the car. By now, Pam's brain was really working. Kate had to tell her to stop talking because it was nothing to that. Will was single but she wouldn't dare cheat on Craig. Pam just wouldn't stop but Kate's attention got back on what she was doing.

She looked down the hall way in the bedroom where she had laid Nikeel and looking for him to be in the middle of the bed but he wasn't. She went running to the bedroom. Pam was behind her. She knew that he could not have crawled, he was only 1 month old. Then Kate could hear a noise like a little cat and it was coming from the other side of the room. Whenever she walked over, Patrice had pulled Nikeel off the bed and put him in the trash.

She knew Patrice had done it because no one else was in the back. Pam was laughing so hard and then Kate remembered what Patrice had said when she was in the hospital. After Kate checked Nikeel to make sure he was ok she called for Patrice, but she wouldn't come. She put Nikeel on the bed and went looking for her, when she found her she was in her room hiding in the closet. Kate took her by the hand and took her back to the room and explained to her how dangerous that was. Patrice said she was sorry. Kate asked her why did she do that and she said because she wasn't the baby anymore. Kate began telling her how the both of them was the baby and how she was going to let her be the big sister to help feed and change him. So it seemed after Kate told her that, she didn't put him in the trash again. Kate told Pam maybe she shouldn't have waited 5 years before they had another baby. Finally Kate got a call from Craig. They talked, but he told her that he could not call that often because it would be very expensive. Kate was getting really bored. Will would come over every day and check on them. She would make dinner and Will would stay and eat. As Kate and Will were sitting down after dinner once, he began telling her how pretty she was and Craig should treat her better. Kate got very upset and told Will that she thought that this was a subject they should not touch. Will was a very good gentleman. He apologized. It was Kate's birthday, Pam wanted them to go out for dinner and drinks. Kate's thought was, that would be nice. Kate got one of their other friends named, Linda to babysit. She wanted kids but it seemed her and Michael could not have any. So when calling Linda she was so excited. She said to bring enough clothes for them to spend the night.

Linda and Michael lived on base also, just a few streets over. Pam and Roy had 3 kids. He was going to keep them. Kate and Pam dropped the kids off. Kate told Linda she would see her the next day. Dinner was great, then they went to a nice club that Pam knew about. Everyone was so friendly. Kate told Pam that Craig had never taken her to a nice place like that. Pam told her to just enjoy herself and they did. It seemed they didn't have to buy any drinks. Some guy was sending them drinks over to their table where they were sitting. Pam told the bartender it was Kate's birthday. Kate was drinking very slowly because she knew Craig was not at home. She told Pam she didn't want to get drunk. She would go on the dance floor to dance. Whenever Kate was going back to her seat, she noticed the guy who was sitting at the table was Will. Kate yells to Pam, "Will is here." Pam laughs, and said, "I know, he is the one that has been sending the drinks." Kate began telling Pam that it may not have been a good idea for her to be there. Pam asked, "why?" Kate told her about the conversation he was trying to have a few weeks before. Pam was like, "Craig would kill him!" Kate said she knows, but he would never know. That had to be their secret. The both of them laughed. But after finding out it was Will that was sending the drinks she got uncomfortable. She was ready to go. Kate told Pam it was getting late. Kate was so glad Will didn't come over to the table. Pam pulled up in her drive way and Kate walked across the street. Her phone rang, Pam says, "just making sure you are in the house." They laughed and hung up. When Kate was walking down the hallway the doorbell rang. She thought it was Pam. As she went to the door she said, "girl what do you want?' When she opened the door, surprisingly, it was Will. He caught her off guard. She asked him why was he there. He told her that he just wanted to make sure she had made it home safely. She told him, "yes." He wanted to know if he could come in. She said, that she guess so. When they sat down Kate told Will, that she didn't think it was a good idea they see each other that time of night. He said, "we all are friends." She let him know, Yeah but she didn't think Craig would appreciate them being together that late. Kate had been feeling that Will liked her ever since they had the conversation about Craig, but she was not for sure. She knew this time by him showing up the way he did, it was true. Kate was very uneasy with Will being there. She had a few drinks and so had Will, but she knew she had to behave herself even though he was good looking, had very warm compassion, was a very smooth talker, he was about 3 years older than her, but she was not going to fall for the game. Even though it was very tempting. She told Will that she would rather for him not to ever come over anymore that time of night. Will told her that she didn't have to worry about him. That he would not ever try anything that she didn't want him to do. Kate mumbled under her breath, "I will be no fool because looking at someone that good looking, temptation would be very easy to get in." Kate told Will that the houses on base were very close and everyone can see who come and goes. And she wouldn't want anyone to tell Craig he was coming over all times of the night. Will reminded her that he had told him to take good care of his family. Kate laughs, and agreed, but reminded Will that, he did tell him to take good care of his family, but he knew and she knew, that he was not talking about in the way that he may have been thinking. Will laughs with a loud laughter and leaned over, as he was standing to leave.

After laying down Kate could not sleep. The next morning Pam came over. Kate was kind of quiet. Pam asked, why was Will at her house. She figured Pam maybe had seen him because she had just hung the phone up from talking to her. Kate thinking in the back of her head, as close as they were she wasn't going to say anything. But after Pam said something to her she told Pam, "yes, he did come over late last night, but never again." She told Pam, that Craig could not every know about this, hoping that Pam never spoke to Roy about it. Pam told Kate, no he was asleep.

Kate said, "good," because Craig and her were already having some problems before he left but she figured with him leaving they just needed a break. As time went on Pam and Kate would go out and they would see Will. He would always come over to the table and speak and send a drink to the table but never came that late at night again. Kate got a telephone call from home, with sad news, learning her grandmother had died. She was very close to her, as she had helped her parents to raise her. This was her father's mother. Her mama called her and told her that her daddy would come to Florida and get her, so she would not have to fly with 2 children. Kate was so glad to hear that but she didn't want her daddy to drive by himself. When talking to him, he laughed, and said, "you know I got my old standby to come with me." His brother—in—law always stuck by him. They were like two peas in a pod, they both were truck drivers after not farming anymore, they delivered furniture from state to state. So her daddy told her that Florida was nowhere to drive. So she said thanks and that her and the kids would be ready. When getting off the phone with her father, she called Will and told him her and the kids would have to leave for a few days. He asked what happened. When she told him, he was so nice, giving his condolences, and asking if there was anything he could do. Kate asked him was there anyway she could contact Craig, so that she could give him the news and also so that she maybe could talk to him before she leaves. Will told her that he would set it up on the base for her to come out and talk to him, and he did just that. When Kate went to the base they called Craig place where he was living, but Kate got very disturbed, a lady answered the telephone. She was speaking a language that Kate could hardly understand. Whenever Craig came to the phone, Kate said hello. She asked him who was

45

the lady that answered the telephone, and he quickly told her, that it was his maid. Kate was trying to except what he was saying. But she knew that times was different from where they were. Kate was holding conversation very slow with him, Craig knew Kate's head was pounding by the minute. And she was thinking the worst, but she kept convincing herself that Craig was not cheating.

Craig's conversation was very short, and not being compassionate at all. Kate was trying very hard not to show any anger at the situation, no tears, or anything that would give away that there was a problem. Just before hanging up, Kate said to Craig, "I love you and miss you" and he never said one word. She just hung up, playing it off that he really said something. Kate left. After a few hours of being home, Kate was packing for them to go to Myrtle Beach, tears ran down her face. Kate had not talked to Pam when she came from the base, she just went home hurting inside like she was going to be sick at any time. When the doorbell rang she thought it was who she could trust, Pam. When opening the door again, it was Will. Kate knew in the back of her mind, wrong answer . . . she didn't need to see him but before she knew it, she was around his neck, closing the door, laying her head on his shoulders, and just sobbing away. Will just held her very tight letting her know that it was ok and he was there for her. Kate looked up at him and said, "that's what I am afraid of." Will asked her what happened on the phone, and she told him. When she did, he looked at her and said that he was so sorry. Kate asked what did he mean? Will looked at her and said that she could never tell Craig that he had told her about this, Craig had wrote him a letter and told him about what kind of friends he had in Japan. Kate began to reminisce and crying much harder and asked was that the reason why his conversations was what they were. At first Will didn't say anything. Then he said, "yes." But it had been more than that. Ever since they were in Austin, he had noticed how Craig would talk to her and treat her. And by him and Craig being friends that he knew that he was attracted to her but he could not let on and now that Craig was in Japan and him writing and telling what he was doing in Japan. He just felt like she deserve better.

Kate told Will that she was glad she was going away for a few days, because, even though her knowing what she knew, that she still couldn't cheat on Craig especially with him. That he and Craig were best friends. Will told Kate that he understood, but again, he had told him to take care of her. Kate just shook her head. Will left and Pam came over. As Kate trying to get her and the kid's clothes packed for her daddy to pick her up the next day. Pam and Kate began talking about the telephone call had she made to Craig. Kate told Pam, that Craig had told her, that the lady that answered the telephone, was his maid. How could this man tell me this, when the time is a totally different time zone. Pam became very angry, asking Kate what was she was going to do. She said, "right now, absolutely nothing." She couldn't let her parents know when she went home. She was just going to concentrate on her grandmother's funeral. And it was going to be nice to get away from Will so she could keep her mind focused. She also had not been home since she took Patrice and now the family was going to see Nikeel. She did not want her family to know about her and Craig. She did not want them to even think they were having these problems because her and Craig had been in love since 8th grade. She thought maybe them being separated from each other, things would get better when they get back together.

The next day Kate's father and uncle came to get her and the kids. She was so glad. They were so happy of course to see her but most of all the kids. Kate's father was really cutting up about Nikeel saying how big a boy he was. He gave him the name Heavy D. The ride was pleasant. Kate again thinking about her mother in the kitchen. And of course she was. Kate and Patrice had not seen everyone in 4 years and then they also were looking at a boy now added to the family. When reaching home, Kate was holding her breath and hoping no one asks about Craig because that was a very sore subject for her to talk about. She knew if she called his mother she had no other choice, but her mother was the first to ask. She just answered her with as short of an answer as she could. Kate was not looking forward to the day of the funeral. Her grandmother was her father's mother and she was a very sweet lady. She loved all her grandchildren, but she helped Kate's parents raise her because Kate's mom became very ill. The funeral was very sad. Everybody knew they would miss her so much. Craig's mom called and wanted to know how long would she be home. Kate knew with her mama and daddy's house being not even 10 minutes away from her mother-n-laws house she had to go over because they have not seen Nikeel either. On Craig's side of the family they were the first grand's. When getting with his family, Kate sort of put everything she was feeling behind her. She began to put in her mind, maybe it was the maid and maybe they had got the time frame wrong. Either way she wanted to have a good stay since she was back home for a few days. Kate did not have a job, so she stayed home for a month. Her and Pam stayed in contact with each other. She would tell Pam to check on things around the house. Pam told her yes, her and Roy was keeping an eye on things. Kate had left a key with Pam to go in and water the plants. Pam with her crazy self could not hold it to tell Kate, that Will had been asking about her, and when was she coming back. Kate told Pam, that now that she was home with her family if she had brought enough clothes for her and the kids they would stay longer. And if she didn't have to buy pampers and milk for Nikeel, maybe she needed to stay there for the next 5 more months, and that it would be that long before Craig came back, so that she could stay out of trouble. Pam and Kate laughed. Pam told her that she was not worried about her doing anything wrong, because that she was such a level headed person. Kate told her, she was hearing what she was saying but she had a husband she loved, but he had been acting kind of strange and he was probably doing God knows what in Japan. And there was a tall black stallion man, with broad shoulders, and grey eyes, that had been noticing her in all kind of ways. He would always smell good every time that she would see him and knew all the right words to say that a woman would want to hear. Kate wanted to know from Pam, how could she think that she was strong enough to fight the feeling? She let Pam know that she was glad she had that much of confidence in her. Kate had to laugh at her own statement. She told Pam she would be letting her know when she would be leaving but for her not to tell Will. Pam agreed with her. Kate stayed a few more days and then her daddy and uncle took her and the kids back. While Kate was riding, she had mixed feelings about going home, but was sure everyone should know how that can be. There is nothing greater than being in your own place. Kate and Pam were so glad to see each other. Kate tried to get her daddy and uncle to stay overnight but he said, "no, they would just rest for a few hours and then leave." He told her and Pam they were used to traveling. After Kate's daddy and uncle left, Pam was still over giving Kate all the details of what had been going on since she left. Kate told Pam that she wished she had a job to keep herself busy. Pam replied and told her she does have a job. (her children)

Kate agreed, but also let her know that at least when a person has a job they can meet people and focus their mind on other things rather than their own personal problems. But she told Pam when she was in Austin, Craig told her he did not want her to work, he wanted her to be a stay at home mom. But she had worked part of her life and has worked on a farm for years, she loved being around people. Days went by and finally Will came by. He wanted to know how long had she been home, and why didn't she call him. Kate was kind of speechless because she knew she really was trying to avoid him. Finally Craig called, he asked her in a very arrogant tone, when did she get back? Kate became very quiet, then telling him that she had only been home for a few hours. She asked him what was going on with their relationship? He told her that they would talk about it when he came home in a few months, and then just changing the conversation immediately, and began asking about the children. Kate wanted to know if he would he be coming home early. He said, "no, but whenever he did come back, that he would be stationed in Virginia." After telling her that it seemed as if it was a long silence from the both of them. Then Craig saying to her that he would call her when he would be arriving back to Ft. Walton Beach, FL. Kate told him ok. After hanging up the phone, she began cooking the kids something to eat, feeding them and then running their bath water to get them ready for bed. As she was doing so she could feel the tears falling down on her cheeks. Thinking, how could something that seemed so right, but also seem as if her life was being pulled right away. Her and Craig seemed to be the lovers that was like a fairy tale. Their classmates would tell them all the time that they thought they were only couple to date from 8th grade and then marry.

The next day Will came over in the afternoon and said to Kate, for her not to cook that afternoon and for her to call Linda and see if she would keep the kids, because he was taking her out for dinner. Kate did not even second guess him, she accepted the invite. She called Linda and of course Linda had no problem keeping them. Will asked her would she like for him to pick her up. Kate told him, no way, that she would meet him. He suggested for her to come by his house and they would leave together. It seemed as though Kate was getting comfortable with the fact, maybe her marriage was not going to continue much longer. But it was not that she had not tried to make it work, but she tried to put in her mind she wasn't going to harp on anything that she couldn't do anything about either. She would just enjoy a friend. She was hoping Pam did not learn she was going out with Will. Even though they were very close she didn't want to be at a point that she would fill like she would have to tell her everything, because she didn't want Pam to put more to the situation than it was. It was just a friendly dinner. As Kate was giving the kids their bath the doorbell rang. It was Pam. Kate opened the door and walked back to the room continuing what she was doing. Hoping Pam was not going to be there very long. After a few minutes she said Roy should be back, she hoped. Kate asked what were they going to do for the night? Pam told her that they had a few people coming over and Roy was going to cook on the grill and just sit around drinking and talking. She asked Kate to come over. Kate told her, "no thanks." Everyone would be coupled off and she would rather not. Of course, Pam was very persistent wanting her to still come. Kate kept a straight face, never letting her know that she was going to meet Will or had other plans.

Boy was she glad when she left. She had to shower and get dressed. After getting ready she called Will and told him she was running a little behind. And of course, he was so polite. She told Will she was not for sure if she remembered where he lived. She had been there many times with Craig but never had been inside. So he gave her directions. But she thought once she got in the neighborhood she could find his house. She let him know that she would see him shortly.

When it was time for her and the kids to get in the car, Kate was hoping that Pam and Roy and their guests were on the back deck of their home so they would not see her leaving. Even when she got dressed she wanted to look her best, but she didn't want Linda's husband Michael to see her and start asking questions. He and Craig did not work in the same building but they still worked on the same base. When reaching Linda's home, Michael was leaving. Kate was relieved because he would not see her when she got out of the car. When she got out of the car and was taking the kids to the door, Patrice began to cry. She had never done that before. She would always love to go to Linda and Michael's house.

Kate asking Patrice what was wrong, but she just kept crying. Kate rang the doorbell, trying to calm Patrice down. When Linda opened the door, she picked Patrice up while she was still crying loudly. Kate put Nikeel down, taking Patrice from Linda and asking her again what was wrong. Patrice just kept crying, Kate began checking her. Patrice had stink in her pants or say her pajamas. Kate knew she would need to be bathed all over again. Linda of course as sweet as she was, she told Kate to go ahead, she would take care of her. She also complimented Kate and told her she looked very nice, that she must have a hot date. Kate laughed and told her, "no, just me and some girls are just meeting to have some drinks." Linda told her that she was surprised to see that Pam was not with her. Kate told her that Pam and Roy had plans. She told Linda that she felt bad to leave Patrice like that and she had to bathe her. Linda told her that she knew it was not a problem because she loved the kids, and they seemed like they were hers. She said Michael was gone for the night, he had to work the night shift. Kate told her thanks and she would not be late.

Kate was finally leaving, later than ever. She didn't understand Patrice stinking in her clothes, she had never done that. But once she had got her calmed down she told her that her stomach was hurting. Kate had to calm herself down because all kind of things were going through her head because Patrice had never cried before when she went to Linda's. Kate thought maybe that was a sign for her not to go and meet Will. But once she found out what was actually wrong, both Patrice and Kate calmed down. At this time Patrice was five years old. Kate tried to put her mind back on what she was suppose to be doing but she knew if something else would had been going on that made Patrice act as if she didn't want to stay with Linda she would not have left them. She finally was in the area. Kate was getting very nervous. She could not find the apartment. She had to go up to the store to a pay phone to call Will to get further directions. When she did, he told her he was getting worried. She apologized for the tardiness, but she would tell him when they saw each other. She told him where she was and she found out she was only a few minutes away. She told him ok. She was still nervous and with the problem that she had with Patrice she had already told herself if she could not find his apartment it was another sign for her not to go. But when she arrived at the door, knocked, thinking he was ready to go, he came to the door in his robe, smelling good, looking good, and Kate is standing at the door speechless. He told her to come in. Kate's body went stiff, and she was lost for words. His place was beautiful. Kate could see in the dinning area, he had it set up for dinner with wine. She sat down because she thought she was going to fall down when he opened the door in his robe. After she had sat for a few minutes and could came back to reality, she jumped up and said she better leave because that was not the kind of night she was prepared for. Will took her by the hand and began massaging them back and forth, telling her to relax, he was not going to take advantage of her. Kate told him that she knew she didn't need to be there because he was not dressed and he knew that would cause temptation. Will apologized again saying, that he did not intentionally come to the door undressed. He explained, that he had taken a bottle of wine down to put on ice, when he popped the cork, that he had spilled wine all over himself, and after she was running late, he thought he had enough of time to shower and dress before she got there. Kate told him how sorry she was for always jumping to conclusions because he has been nothing but a gentleman. He then asked her would she excuse him for a minute while he go and put some clothes on. Kate said, yes. As Will was going to the bedroom, Kate didn't know what she wanted to do, run to the front door and leave or follow him into the bedroom, all kinds of things were exploring through her mind, head spinning, and thinking about what was behind that closed door. But she had to quickly pull it together, if she was going to stay, because she could not give him any idea how she felt about him. Whenever Will came out, he was dressed in some jeans and a nice shirt. Kate took her eyes off of him real quickly. He told her to come to the table. When she got ready to sit down, he pulled out the chair for her to sit down, and the sent/smell of the cologne he wore, would take your breath away.(he smelled so good) Kate looked up at him and thanked him. He brought her a very nice salad out first. After eating their salad, he then brought in a nice steak and baked potato and poured them some wine in some nice wine glasses. After such a romantic dinner, he pulled Kate's chair out so she could get up and move to the sofa. When she stood up, she felt so light headed. So Will took her by the hand and walked her to the chair. Again she felt that she was no drinker, but it seemed the wine was very strong. After she was comfortable on the chair, Will went back in the dinning area and started cleaning up the dishes.

After cleaning up so nicely, everything looked so good for him being a man and living by himself. He sat down by Kate and she told him she would be leaving because it was getting late and she didn't want to go to the club. Will told her that she knew that was the time everybody goes out (late). Kate agreed, but because she was feeling a little light headed she didn't want to go anywhere but to her bed. He told her, as his hands are still massaging her shoulders, for her to just relax for a little while. Kate took a long breath and began to cry. Will, being the gentleman that he was reached over and held her in his arms. Kate told him she felt so comfortable with him, but she knew it was wrong because of being married to Craig. As she laid and sobbed for a little while on his shoulder, Kate looked up at Will and told him that she could easily do the wrong thing but she felt she was gong to behave herself because she was going to wait it out until Craig came home. An as she would wait for him to come home at the same time she would hope things would be different when he did get back home because if not she would have been a fool to let him get away. They laughed and with him saying that he could tell Craig that she was a real woman and he needed to take care and love her right. Kate was getting sleepy so she was going to leave and it was also late. She was glad to know Michael was working the late shift and he wouldn't be there when she picked the kids up. Will walked her to the car, making sure she got off good. Kate was so nervous and was looking over her shoulder, worrying about who might be looking. Will tried to insure her that she had nothing to worry about. Finally Kate was in her car on the way home. She just cried and cried, because she knew it was just an honest dinner but she knew it could have been a situation she didn't want to feel bad about, commiting adultery.

When getting to Linda's house to get the kids she tried to wipe her eyes so Linda would not ask any questions. Linda was very quiet, she was nothing like Pam. She would have been grilling her with all sorts of questions. Kate rang the doorbell, waking Linda up. Linda opened the door, asking how was the night and that was the extent of her questions and Kate was so glad. When driving home, she knew she would have been ok because everybody should have been sleeping. Especially Pam and Roy, as they lived directly across the street from her. After arriving home Kate felt she could breathe again, there was no lights on over at Pam's house and none of their company was still there. As Kate was getting the kids in and settled, she just sat down on the bed and began to cry again. Thinking about what she had just participated in, even though it was just a friendly dinner. While taking her clothes off, she was thinking how she would be glad that she had only a few months left. She laid across the bed falling asleep and drowning in her tears. The next morning came and who was at the door early morning before Kate and the kids were up. She goes to the door and it's Pam, with all of her questions. She was just laughing inside because she already knew Pam was going to do it. Pam was a good friend but Kate would tell her that she was too nosey at times. Of course Pam didn't care, she was just crazy. Kate told her to wait for her to wake up and at least wash her face before she drilled her with a million questions. They laughed, Pam said, "girl I seen you when you were leaving, you had on that bad black dress that we bought at the mall last month." Kate just kept doing what she was doing, which was making them a pot of coffee. While the kids were still asleep they both got a cup of coffee while sitting at the table. Kate said nothing at first. Pam instigating and going on and on. Kate just laughing at her and told her, "girl you probably did not even fix your family breakfast." That she had came over there early to get some gossip. She just laughed and asked, "who did you go out with?" Pam was a great friend, she felt she could trust her and also because knew some stories on her. She had no conscience, she had cheated on Roy before and she told Kate her secrets. And she knew also that she could not lie to her where she would believe she had went out with some other girls.

Because she knew Kate had only been around a few people, but she only went out with her. So Kate finally looks at her and said, "Will." When she did, Pam jumps up like a little child talking about, "girl, I should have known that is who/why you were wearing that black dress." They just laughed and laughed. Kate gives her the hold IN-4. When Pam heard the story she told Kate, that she had to be lying. That she had went to this man house, him being as fine as he was, and her looking like Halle Berry, and of course Kate stopped her and reminded her that she knows, she does not look no where close to her. Pam says girl, "I have told you about putting yourself down." She also told her that, she was a pretty young lady, she has a few pounds that she could loose, but she has to understand that whenever she dress up, she can look like whoever she want to be. Kate said, "well that's me." Pam told her that she was joking around, but seriously she did look nice in the dress. It was her size and everything was in place. And she bet Will thought so too. Kate is laughing like crazy at Pam. She said some men love some meat on their bones and some love theirs a little boney and a little meat.

Pam says, "now getting back to Will, you mean to tell me, that man didn't throw you down?" Kate's looking at her just shaking her head. Pam asked, "girl, is the man gay or, are you a lesbian?" Kate told her, "no!" "girl, it's not like that it could not have happened, but I am married to Craig and Will is Craig's best friend, and besides it would mess up their friendship for life." And that she really did not buy the story about the wine spilling all over him, she believed it was a set up. But whenever he found out that she was not all over him, or making any sexual advances towards him, he got dressed. He had always been a gentleman, he respects her also. Girl everybody is not like you with your crazy self. They laughed and changed the subject. Kate told her that Craig should be calling in a few days and coming home. And sure enough Will came over that afternoon and said he had received a call on the base from Craig saying that he would be coming home in 2 weeks and he wanted him to drive her and the kids to the airport. Kate asked him wasn't he glad nothing really happened between them and knowing they had to ride again to the airport together. He said, "yes and no." Because he knew his and Craig's conversations. Kate said she knows, but it would be worse if they had slept together. This way they really didn't have anything to worry about or be accused of. Craig called Kate a few days later telling her the same thing about, Will would be picking him up, the time, and that he would be glad to see them. Kate was feeling so good to hear him say that. She told Will she was so glad she was innocent with everything while he was gone.

When Kate told crazy Pam about Craig coming home she was like, "oh no I won't see my friend for awhile." Kate laughs and asked her what did she think? She also told Pam that she was so glad she was innocent while he was gone. That fool fell back on the chair laughing like she didn't have good sense. Kate asked her what was wrong with her. She said that there was nothing innocent about her or Will. They were just two fools who just didn't do what she would have done. They had came so close and all the feelings were there, but as she had said he was a gentleman. He was bald headed and his brain must could not functioning properly. And as for Kate, she had always told her about keeping her hair pinned up. Her hair must have been too tight. Cause if that had been her, (Pam), well, she didn't need to say anymore. Kate replied, "no please don't." Pam kept something going all the time, there was not a boring moment.

The day had come to pick Craig up from the airport. Will came over and they put Patrice and Nikeel in the car. Patrice, she was saying over and over, " I'm going to see my daddy." Nikeel he didn't know who he was because he was only 2 months old when Craig left. So he would just say dad, dad. Kate gets in the car and of course, Will opening the door. As Kate is fastening her seat belt and Will is backing the car out, she took a long deep breath, in hopes that when picking Craig up it was going to be everything she wanted it to be. She had wore that black dress. Will telling her again how nice she looked, but this time Kate not even really wanting to take any compliments from him, she wanted to keep her mind focused on Craig, so Kate was very quiet. Will was a great person to be around, but he gave Kate her space. When arriving at the airport Kate was getting very excited to see Craig. They got out of the car. Will get's Patrice and Kate get's Nikeel. After they got inside the airport to find out they had to wait for his flight. Again there is little words spoken between the two of them. Then Will spoke and said, "well his flight is here." Kate stood up holding Nikeel and Patrice standing beside her.

When Craig got closer Patrice turned Kate's hand loose and went running and jumped in her daddy's arms. Craig walks over and takes Nikeel from Kate, holding him very close, and saying, "my man." Kate is standing there waiting for a hug and a kiss. He walked by her and walked over to Will and done the hand shake that men do. Then he turns to Kate and said hey and walked off with the kids. Kate was standing there with her mouth open, thinking and saying to herself, "this can't be happening." Will was standing there looking as if he could just pull Kate close to him, but he knew he couldn't. Kate just walked very slowly behind them. When reaching the car, she got in the backseat with the kids. Will said to her that he would sit in the back with the kids. Craig told Will, "man, no, let her sit in the back." Kate's feelings were so hurt. They had not seen each other in a year and one month and this was the way she was getting treated. When getting home Kate just got out of the car, went in the house, and changed her clothes. Craig was still outside with the kids and talking to Will, Kate came back outside and said, "excuse me, I'm leaving for a while." Craig never really looked up at her, him and Will just moved away from the car and Kate left. After getting to a store where she could get to a pay phone, she called Pam. Kate was crying her eye balls out. Pam answers the phone all crazy of course, saying crazy things then when she really took time to breathe she heard Kate's voice. She asked, "what's wrong?" Kate told her she couldn't tell her over the phone. She told Kate to tell her where she wanted her to meet her at. Pam told her to give her a few minutes because she was feeding her family. She told her ok. As Kate was sitting in the restaurant, she thought about that, she had taken steaks out and potatoes to bake for her and Craig after getting the kids settled. Trying to have a romantic evening, and enjoy him being back home. But she just left because she was so hurt and she knew Will was thinking the worse right now, because he tried to tell her. But because she loved her husband, she was still trying to blank out what had just happened at the airport. But it was hard to do when that crazy Pam came in and whenever she had told her what had happened at the airport. That nut jumps up and say, "let's call Will!" Kate told her, "no way, was she crazy?" She said, "yeah, because I want my friend to be taken care of. Do you know what I mean?" Kate told her yes, but that was not the way she was going to do it, she just needed to leave for a few minutes to exhale and who else could she have called but her best friend. Pam told her that Will was her best friend too and he could help her better. Kate just looks at her and laughs and says, "you are sick." And that she had called her because she needed someone to confine in. That crazy girl just wouldn't stop she said, to let her remind me that he did tell you to let Will take care of you. Kate told her that he did not mean like that Pam. After they sat there for a while and chatted, Kate finally told her she was ready to go back. She was going to stop and get a bottle of wine and go home and get the kids settled and then maybe they could have a nice evening. Pam told her that maybe her and Roy would come by so she could have a good night. Kate told her to let them try things by themselves for the night. Before Craig went off to Japan Pam and Roy would come over and they would have a great time. They would play spades. And just being around Pam as you have read thus far you should be able to tell that she is a mess all by herself. Roy is worst because he have to say things to keep up with her. But they were all together great people. Kate stopped and got the wine so that would give Pam time to get home before her, so it wouldn't look like they had been together. She walked in the house and the kids and Craig were asleep. Kate woke Craig up, when she went in the kitchen. He came in behind her and asked where had she been? Kate starting to tell him where she had been and the reason why she left. But before she could finish, he told her to not worry about explaining because he really didn't care. Kate stood there in shock and looking at him. Then she told him that she didn't know what was wrong with him, but she would not continue to live like that. She said that she thought that them taking a break from each other for a year that it would make a difference. She just couldn't understand the drastic change in him. As soon as Jan had showed her how to drive and she also started going out every now and then with her, he had changed. He had been going out with the guys when he wanted to and have them over and she had never complained not one time. Craig got up from the chair and told her, "you are right, I'm the man." When she had started doing things, Jan wanted her to do, then things changed with them. Kate told him how unfair he was being. And put in his remembrance that it was her birthday and that he had told Jan to take her out and he would stay home with Patrice. But she see's where this was going. She told him, "you don't have control of me anymore, that's why you didn't want me to learn how to drive." She said that she thought he really love her. Craig said nothing. She also told him maybe she better go home. He told her, she might as well wait because they would be leaving the base where they were in a few weeks because he had got orders to Virginia. Kate left boiling her eyes out. The next day Craig must have told Will about the situation because while Will was on break at work, he called Kate. She asked him, where was Craig? He made a bad comment. In the past, and most of the time when anyone would say anything about Craig, Kate would take up or defend him. She won't let anyone say anything bad about him. Will told Kate he wanted her to meet him at the restaurant across town. She told him ok. Before hanging up Will said, "I love you." Kate began to cry like crazy. He asked if she was ok? She said no, but she would be and then hung up. When hanging up, her cry became louder and louder. She finally got enough strength to dial Pam to ask her to come over. She was lucky her kids were in school, her kids was her life. When Pam got there Kate was still crying. Pam asked what has . . . done now. You can imagine what she said.(the dotted line) Craig didn't like Pam at all because she was very out spoken. He said that he thought with me hanging with her, when he got back he was waiting to hear how I had been with different men. But little did he know she didn't care for him either. Kate told her what Craig had said the night before, but why she was really crying was because of the fact, here is a man she loved so much, he had been gone for a year, and he had not touched her since he had been back home from deployment, he has not said that he missed her or love her, and then here is another man, all they have done, was spend time together, laughing, and dinning together, and he had told her that he loves her. Pam jumped up and looks at

Kate and tells her, "leave that fool." Kate agreed and told her maybe she was right. She was going to meet with Will that tonight across town so she was going to give her a number whenever she would get where she was going to be, so if she seen him leaving the house, she needed to call her. Even though he would have the kids, she was sure he won't leave, but then you never know. Now Pam is already geared up. She was already for the move of Kate. They continued their conversation and then it was getting late in the afternoon.

So Kate told Pam she wanted to start dinner. Pam was one of those Louisiana women, Roy had hell on his hands. But they had a great relationship, that's why Kate asked her why would she cheat on him? Her response was that, she was drinking and she was in the wrong place at the wrong time. She said she felt very bad for doing it. Well Kate went on cooking dinner. When Craig got home he walked in, no kiss, or nothing, and barely speaking. Walking over to Patrice and picking Nikeel up. Meanwhile Kate was doing all she could do to hold a conversation but he was not budging. He just kept his attention on the kids. After Kate was finished with dinner she had Patrice to come to the table and put Nikeel in the high chair and help with feeding him. Afterwards Kate gave the kids their bath. Craig was reclined in his chair. Kate put the kids down then began getting herself dressed. When dressed she walked out in front of Craig so he could see her real good. When standing in front of him, she knew that if nothing else, the smell of her perfume should have woke him up. But he laid still as if he didn't see or hear her. She knew he had to know she was standing there but he was being very stubborn. She walked over and kisses the kids when doing so, he rises up and look very wide eyed at her and asked, "where are you going?" Kate only in answer saying, "out for a while." He told her that he guessed that she and Pam had to go do what they do best. Kate looked at him and asked what was that suppose to mean? And saying nothing else. She walked out the door, smiling inside, and thinking, "you think that it's with Pam." As she backed out of the drive way, she noticed Craig standing in the kitchen window looking and he never saw Pam get in the car. When she arrived at the restaurant, Will was sitting inside waiting for her. She got out of the car, and walked in. Will does the gentleman thing, he pulls the chair out for her to sit, he takes Kate by her hand, and he let her know that he knew she was hurting, and her heart was burden. Kate didn't say anything she just sat and listened. He then told her that he was so sorry, but that Craig was a butt hole. That he was so cocky and arrogant, he wanted her to know that she didn't have to stay with someone like that. Kate finally saying something with tears in her eyes. She said that she has two children. Will interrupted her, "and!" Kate told him that she wanted her marriage to work, but she didn't think Craig wanted the same. That he had not said it, but his actions says it. Will told her the reason he asked her to come to the restaurant was, he wanted also to let her know that she could stay in Florida when Craig got ready to go to Virginia. Kate was speechless. She asked Will where and what would he do about his girlfriend? He said he didn't have one, since he had came to Florida. The girl that he had been dating in Austin, Texas did not work out and therefore she had no reason to come along. Kate said she didn't understand, that he was too nice and she didn't want to be a smother and what would she give to have all that back? That's the way Craig used to be. Will told Kate, the reason that he did not get involved with anyone there, was because he knew he had a crush on her.

And because he and Craig were working in the same department and every since he had visited their home in Texas and saw how he was treating her, that he didn't like it. Then when they got orders to Florida and they would be stationed in Florida together he was not going to date anyone. He was going to see where his relationship with her could go because Craig was telling him about what he was doing in Japan. He also told her that he knew that he was going to act like that because he was so involved with the woman over there. (Japan)

Kate told Will all of that he was saying was so sweet, but she had never been or even thought she would be treated like that. She told Will that she wouldn't be able to stay there with the kids because she knew that Craig would never let that happen, because he had already been gone a little more than a year from the kids and he loved them. And she knew she love them and she would never let him have her children. Will told her that he know that she was a good woman that's why he didn't want to see her hurting.

Kate reminded him that just in a few days the movers would be coming to pack. Will said he knew, but he wanted her to know that if she needed to come back, her and the kids, didn't have to worry about anything, just call. Kate told Will, "how could something so wrong, feel so right?" She told him that she best get back home. He didn't' want her to leave. She never thought she would say this to Will, "but if it was not for my children I would not go back home." As Kate drove home, it seemed she was dreading every mile, hoping that whenever she would get home, that Craig would already be in bed. When reaching home Craig was still in his chair watching T.V. Kate walked in and passed no words. She went on down the hall way. Craig sat up and called her name. Kate turns back around and walks back up where Craig was and says, "yes." He asked, "where and who have you been with?" Kate just stood looking puzzled. He says, "and don't tell me that you were with Pam."

Kate smiling inside but never letting Craig see that because he had been acting like he didn't care. She said, "no I was not with Pam," she had went by herself because she needed some me time. He looked all crazy and bugged eyed and asked what did she mean by that? In Kate's mind, she was thinking, he acted as if he did not care, but maybe this got his attention. Kate looked at him and said, "Craig you need to think about what do you want to do with our marriage, because she would not be going to Virginia." So he told her he would let her know. Time passed for them to say good bye. As Kate would always say that's the hardest part of the military life, getting to know some people and then have to depart from each other. And meeting someone like Pam, it was hard to say good bye. And then there was Will, a very close friend.

And Craig finding out that most of their stationed place was going to be separated. So he and Will would not be stationed together at the next base and when Kate thought about it, maybe that was best. Kate and Craig said their good byes and they left for Myrtle Beach. The drive was ok, not the best but she was glad for the little attention she was getting from him. It was better than not getting any at all. When getting to Myrtle Beach they went to his mother's first. He had lost his father after he and Kate had been married for about 3 years. They would go back and forth because Kate's parent's home was not far away. After being at home for about 3 weeks Kate told Craig the surprise of his life. She would make the decision for him since it seemed every time she would bring it up he did not want to talk about it. She would stay with her parents and give him a chance to think about what he wanted. Kate felt that she would be gambling with her marriage if she didn't go because if he had cheated on her before he would do it again but she told him if he did, she would divorce him and move on with her life.

Craig was so shocked. He began to tell her how and why he was not touching her. Kate was very disturbed, she told him that it was best that she stayed with her parents, but she did not want the family to know what was going on. So Craig agreed, even though now that he had come clear in what was going on he knew that Kate maybe would not come to Virginia. So Kate told her parents that her and the kids would be staying behind. They were fine with it, because the only thing they thought was that her and the kids could not leave with Craig because of housing.

Tweety Bird was the baby, so she was excited to know her big sister was going to be home for a little while. Craig became nice all of a sudden. He told Kate he would leave the car with her and he would take the bus on to Virginia. She was glad to hear that. She took him to the bus station and after he arrived in Virginia he called back and said he made it there with no problem. What Kate did was kept a very low profile on how she was really feeling about their relationship because she did not want to gather hopes.

Of course not confiding in no one at home what was going on made her continue to staying in contact with Will, to keep her mind from being so much on Craig. The more she tried and would to talk to Will, the more Craig started calling and paying more attention to her. Something bad happened, Kate got into a bad accident and when Craig got the call he came back home. She was fine, but the car was a total lost. Kate was so shocked how Craig seemed to be changing back to the old Craig she used to know. So she stopped calling Will and began talking to Craig more. After he went back to Virginia and got another car he came after Kate and the kids. He had already moved down town and had everything placed in the home when they arrived. Kate felt like things were looking better for them, so she forgave him. After being in Virginia, maybe for 3 or 4 months they started deployments. Kate started looking for a job. And she was hired at Hardees as their breakfast manager. Patrice was in school and she had to put Nikeel in daycare. Kate and Craig only stayed in Virginia for 2 ½ years, but during this time of being there Tweety Bird was having a baby and she wanted to come and stay with Kate for a little while. Kate was glad to have her company. Craig was gone, so she would have a babysitter for Nikeel. Then she had to leave, so that she could have her baby. The day came for Craig to come home, in finding out the next orders he would be going was to Germany. Kate told him she didn't want to go over there because she had heard so many stories. But Craig assured her that things would not be that way for them, because he had learned enough from being in Japan. One of the stories that Kate had heard was that the American men would take their women over there and end up divorcing their woman and getting the German women and bringing them back to the states. Kate and Craig talked and talked about it. She finally was convinced that she would go. Then the day before they were to leave, Craig got a phone call that Tweety Bird's baby had died. Craig had planned to wait until they got in Germany before he was going to tell Kate what happened. But she overheard him telling a couple that was supposed to take them to the airport. She then fell to her knees saying, "no the baby was only 5 months old." She began asking Craig questions. Kate asked Craig didn't he think that was something that he should have been telling her before they left Virginia? He told her that her mother had said not to tell her until they were in Germany. Kate was very upset, but she could no longer be with Craig. She called home and talked to her mother first. She did tell her that she had told Craig not to tell her until later. But Kate told her she was glad she overheard the conversation. She asked to speak to Tweety Bird and as soon as Tweety Bird heard her voice she began to cry. Kate told her she was so sorry and she would not go to Germany with Craig, she would go later. Tweety Bird told her, "no," that she would be alright. There was nothing she could do. After hanging up with Tweety Bird, Kate told Craig it would have been harder for her to accept the death of Tweety's baby if she had been in Germany. They were leaving Virginia and landing in New York finding out they had to wait for 3 hours before a flight would be going out of New York. Kate was just sitting and enjoying letting Craig do everything because the airport brought back memories of Atlanta. It looked just as big or bigger. Then finding out they had to take several trains before they could get to the gate for departure. Kate was so glad she was experiencing this with Craig because she said if she had waited she would have never went.

Chapter 4

Craig, Kate and the kids are finally reaching Germany after 4 hours in the air. But what a flight. Once in the air you got cotton to put in your ears. The plane again a 747, top and bottom, T.V. set to look at, bar, snacks and then dinner. What great treatment did they get. Patrice and the other kids got coloring books and crayons. Kate could say it was beautiful. After getting there and getting in a taxi, not knowing anything he was saying, Kate knew then, that she was getting ready to experience some things.

While Craig and Kate were in route Craig called his Command Officer on the base. He told him that the base was very small so they had made preparation at a motel. He told him which place and once they were settled they would be by to give them a welcome to the base. Kate was looking so hard saying everything looks so different than the United States. When reaching the motel Kate was amazed how they had 2 rooms, and they were connected to one to the other. They were able to walk out of one door to the other doors with the kids but as she was checking everything out she realized there were no bathrooms in the rooms. She began yelling to Craig asking, "where is the bathroom." She noticed he was not in the room. When he came back to the room she found out there was just one bathroom for all the people in the motel. Kate knew she was not going to like that. Craig was off still for a week before he had to go to work.

Kate and Craig seemed to be gaining their strong relationship back. He was talking more, but the best thing was, he asked Kate to forgive him, and it seemed he really meant it. She was so glad that her and Craig were getting along because trying to deal with the German culture was not working to good. Going in the grocery stores not knowing what they were saying, walking up to the kids and they would put their hands in their kid's faces was getting frustrating for her because Patrice and Nikeel would cry sometimes and it would become difficult sometimes to settle them down. When telling some of the Americans in the motel they told them that Germans were very friendly people. Kate of course, she didn't want to hear that when it came to her kids. Craig told her that things were going to be very different over there. Craig finally had to go to work. Kate and the kids would get up in the mornings and having to go down the hallway to use the bathroom and to bathe. Kate did not like that at all. She was hoping it would be very soon that they would be moving out of the motel. Since the base was very small she knew they would be getting a home downtown. And boy could you tell the Americans home living from the Germans home living by the windows. Kate and Craig lucked up. They got an apartment right downtown. Craig was ready to move Kate and the kids because Kate had been crying for about a month about the motel. Craig told Kate if they did not hurry and find somewhere to go that he was going to have to put her and the kids back on a plane. Kate told Craig he was not going to get any argument from her because it was a lot to get used to. But now that they had the apartment she got excited. After moving in the apartment, Kate then had to get used to cooking the German food because while they were in the motel they ate in the restaurant, where the dogs are welcome also. Craig and the movers were getting the beds and everything set up. Patrice and Nikeel doing what kids do as they had not a care in the world. Kate told Craig since the kids would be in school that she wanted to apply for a job on the base. He told her he didn't think she would be able to get a job because the base was so small. But Kate did not listen she felt she had to do something. Not knowing anybody and she couldn't call home, it would cost so much. Believe it or not, it was not long after she applied she got a call to work in the accounting office downstairs in the main club on the base.

Patrice was seven and Nikeel was three. She would be going to public school with the Germans and Nikeel would go to the daycare on the base. Craig was glad also to find out that Kate would be going to work. Kate was working in accounting. Craig would drop her off at her job first. The weather was very unpredictable, the sun could be shinning one minute then you may look out the window and snow flakes are just dropping. Kate and Craig was getting very used to the culture, everything seemed to be going great. Kate wanted to get her drivers license over there. However, when Craig went to take the test, he told her there were two hundred—fifty questions on the test. Even though he had studied, he had to go three times before he actually past the test. Kate knew it had to be very hard because when Craig was in school he would pass any test he took. Therefore Kate felt she had no chance but she had to try because you could not drive over there unless you had the German license. There was no speed limit to drive. After Craig got his license he was so excited he could go and get a car. They went to look and it was great because everything was very cheap. Kate was loving the fact the cost of living was not too expensive. Their landlord was the best, they fell in love with the kids, but they would have to watch them when they come by to collect the rent. They would take the kids down to the store and give them dinner which was ok but they gave the kids beer to drink. This was the culture over there. Craig told Kate if she would go and try for her license and she got them he would buy her a car. Kate thought to herself, he probably felt she would never be able to get the license. But she would go to work, come home and cook dinner when she had to, and then get the kids to bed. She would then take 2 hours out of each night and study. Then she struck bad and told him she was ready to go try for her license. Craig was shocked. He started teasing her, and asking, "are you sure?" Kate told him, "yes." Kate went stepping to the building after getting out of the car, telling Craig she would walk over to work when she got out. When she entered into the building, there were so many Americans. They were walking out saying, the test was too hard. After she heard so many complaining she tried not to listen to everyone's complaints. Craig was right, there was two hundred—fifty questions. You could get fifty wrong and still pass. When she first sat down, it seemed everything was going to be ok but as she went further down the line, the questions got tough, it seemed as if her mind was coming to a blank. Then there was one hundred signs on the test, the best part about the test, was that they would give you all the time you needed for testing. When she got up she didn't feel she had did that good. When the officer checked her test he told her that she had missed fifty questions and fifty signs. He told her that she could come back in two weeks, she could try again. When Kate got to work one of the girls said to her, "your husband has been calling you." Kate laughs out loud and told them she know, because she had been to try for her license. The girls in the office laughed and said you might as well don't worry about trying to get your license because they all had been and they had not got theirs. Kate told them how many she had missed. One of the girls asked, "are you going back?" she told her, "yes," and that she was not going to stop until she got them. Craig finally called back, getting Kate on the phone, asking the question and waiting for her answer. She just started laughing and telling him she would tell him when she got home. Craig said ok but it was killing him to know if she had passed. As the day went by, that was the talk in the office. But Kate told them she was not going to be a quitter. When Craig picked her up from work, he could not stand it any longer to hear the answer, Kate told him. He told her the same thing all of her coworkers had said to her, that she could never do it. Craig told her that all the guys in the department said that their wives went to try and never went back after the first time. Kate told Craig, that she was going back. Those guys did not encourage their wives to go back but she was not going to be a quitter. And that he was going to be the first sergeant to have a wife to get her license. Craig still didn't seem as if he had a lot of confidence in her. But she did not stop, she believed in herself. It took her going five times but she finally got them. The girls in the office told her, they would not have kept going. Their husbands told them they were embarrassed if they would have kept going and missing so many questions.

Kate told them, well Craig maybe have felt the same way, but she was very independent. She has always been that way, that's the way her parents had raised her. She told the girls, "do you know how it is going to feel to show Craig that she had did it?" The girls told her they could only imagine. They began saying they would go back. Kate thought about if Craig had to be deployed she didn't want to have to call a cab to get around. She could not wait for work to get over. When Craig picked her up from work, he was waiting for her to have a long face like usual. She got in the car smiling; the first words he says is, "I know you couldn't have got your license?" She just kept smiling, because he had already told her, because it was her fifth time if she didn't get them, please do not go back anymore. She just kept smiling, letting him make his little comments. When they got home and they were settled, she laid the license up on the table. Craig walked by the table, and at first he did not see the license. Then he hollered "oh no!, this can't be." Kate was in the kitchen starting dinner. Patrice asked what was wrong, Craig showed her the license, then told her that they must have gave them to her mother. The both of them was just laughing and Kate started laughing right along with them. She told them, "maybe so, if he got tired of me coming in, but she was so glad." Also said that maybe she had gotten on his nerves and that he went ahead and gave them to her, but at least she had got them. She told Craig she encouraged the girls in her office to go back because it is a lot to remember but the guys should want them to be very independent, being that we are in a foreign country. Craig looked at Kate and told her that he was sorry and that she was right. He then let that old ego come out and said when he would go to work the next day he could tell them his baby got her license. Kate just shook her head. After going back to work after a few days Kate's coworkers began telling her how their husbands said Craig acted. But only one of the girls was willing to go and try and when she did she had to go three more times but she finally got them. Yes the test was hard, with two hundred—fifty questions to remember, but we were so happy she went back. Craig had to be a standup guy, he had to buy Kate's car, as he had promised, if she had got her license. So he went out and got her a Volkswagen. He already had one, his was yellow and Kate's was white. She was so excited to get it on the road but she took the slow routes until she learned the big roads because over in Germany there was no speed limit. Craig loved that. She got used to the roads to travel great distances. When going to work she would get so upset because she would have to park the car in one parking lot and then walk to her office.

And if they were walking and they start singing the national anthem they would have to stop. One morning Kate was walking in her heels and got ready to stop, when she did, her heel broke and she went sliding on down because they were going down a hill. She fell, and no one could help her until the national anthem was over. She just laid there quietly. When they had finished, the men that were standing around, came running, of course Kate, she laid there like she was really hurt. When she got up and got to the office everyone was laughing. Come to find out they had been looking out the window at her. One of the girls told everybody, that when Kate went tumbling down, she was smiling, and when the guys got there she started crying and looking real pitiful. Kate looked at the girl and laughed and said, "what would you do if your heel broke?" Kate enjoyed her accounting job. But one of the managers of the club asked her would she be willing to take a job of management of being a bartender. She had been working in the accounting office for a year but they wanted her to become a bartender. She told them she would have to talk to Craig about it before she could give them an answer. Kate wanted to do everything right. Her and Craig had been getting along very good since they had been in Germany. So she went home and her and Craig began talking about it, she explained to Craig what she would be doing. She told him that he knows that she will be around a

77

lot of guys and she will have to wear tops that show the cleavage and short skirts and tight pants. Craig looked at Kate and told her, well that was fine as long as no one would be touching her. He also said that he see's what happens when those other bartenders do and they get great tips. Kate asked Craig if he was sure. He told her yes. Well Kate went back and told them yes. She became a bartender manager. She didn't have to make any drinks at first. She had to observe the other bartenders for a week. Then after learning how to pour the drinks she then had to bartend. As time went by, Kate realized that she was spending more time at the club than at home. She told Craig she was so sorry but she started seeing that behavior that she had seen in Texas and Florida. He would enjoy spending the tips, but his attitude started being very crazy. When he would get off work he had been picking Patrice and Nikeel up and spending time with them. Then he stopped spending time with the kids. He would come to the club and sit at the bar and watch her and make sure no one talked to her too long. She would have to stay until the club closed and lock up. There was always another manager on duty to close at night with her, which was a man.

Kate and Craig would end up arguing every day. She became very upset because she had asked Craig if he was ok about her taking the bar manager job. She started wishing that she had kept her accounting job, to keep confusion down. Then she also thought about Craig saying that he was ok with her taking the job. She did not quit. She started getting a babysitter for the kids because Craig started threatening her about quitting because she would have to stay home with the kids. She told him how unfair he was. But Craig did not want to hear it. Kate went on enjoying her job and then Craig got that much crazier, he stop coming around the club. Kate would not see him sometime until the next day because when she would get home he would not be there and when he did get home, she would already be asleep. Kate tried to talk to him on different occasions. She began to live her life like they were not married. There was plenty of guys she was working with that wanted to talk to her but she was not interested in no one on her job. She also knew she really did not want to cheat on Craig but she knew this time she was not going to put up with his attitude and foolish actions again, especially when he told her he was ok with her accepting the job. She told him he was just going through some jealous rage for no reason because she loved him and if it seemed there was a lot of flirting, that's all it was, because he knew he did not have anything to worry about. She asked him the question, "when I leave the club at night, where and who, do I come home to?" Craig still did not seem to want to listen. So Kate went on enjoying what she was doing. She finally found another person the image of Will, his name was Andrew, he was four years older than her, he was so polite, and everything or more than Will. Then what she loved about it, they did not work together. Kate and Craig began not getting along at all. She had no family to turn to. She was so far from home, but when Andrew came into her life she really was enjoying life. She told Andrew what she had been through with Craig, the status, and how he promised he would never take her through this again. Andrew was so much of a gentlemen Kate would ask him was he sure that his name was not Will. And that maybe he had gotten a face lift. He would laugh. Everything was going great. Kate was so happy again, but the only problem was it was not with Craig. But she learned how to live with it. She then was offered a job to be a D.J. The club owner told her she had the personality to do it. Kate told him she didn't know about that.

He told her to think about it. She would be at the club those nights managing which would be Thursday night was ladies night and then she would have to do it on Friday and Saturday night. He told her they would be giving her a raise. Well, here she goes again, trying to give Craig the benefit of the doubt, even though they were not getting along. She told the owner she would get back to him. She goes home to talk to Craig. When Kate call to Craig so that she could talk, he yells and says in a tone that she knew she did not want to talk to him. She just said, "never mind." He continues to get dressed to leave. A woman knows her man if they are cheating, the wife is the first to know. Craig would never say it. She looked at him saying nothing. After his leaving, she calls Andrew and shared with him what the owner said. Andrew told her, if she feel this was something she thinks she would enjoy, to go for it. So when Kate got to work the next afternoon, she would accept the position. The owner told her he was glad to have her to do that because they needed someone to keep the people busy/entertained. He had her to go to his office and explained what he would be expecting from her and about her raise. When she finished talking with him the job really was very simple. You mainly have to play music to the crowd. She was also informed that the guys they had been using in the past, did not do anything for the crowd. And she knew that because she would be there and would hear a lot of complaints. The owner told her that when he would come by and she had to help work the bar he saw a lot of potential in her. She was real friendly and knew how to deal with people. He told her that he would come in and she never knew he was there. Kate just laughed. He told her to think of a name that she would like to call herself as a DJ. Her name would go on a billboard. Kate told him ok. Kate called Andrew all excited. He was just laughing because she was so excited.

He told her that he knew she would do good and think of a great name. She thought for a moment, how she knew Craig would not like it when he found out what was going on. But when she tried to talk to him he was so busy in his life that she and the kids had to take what they could get. But she was ok. She would get the landlord to watch the kids. She and her husband enjoyed and loved Patrice and Nikeel. They had them spoiled. Kate came up with her D.J. name. Her name was, Lady K. When she told Andrew, he told her that was a great name. So when Kate got to work she gave the owner her information. He was very pleased with her name choice. She was so happy to hear that. The first night for her to D.J., her name was on the billboard. They put it on there on a Monday so the soldiers would know what was going on at the club. When anyone would arrive at the entrance of the base, the billboard was the first thing they would see. Kate and Andrew was having a field day laughing because Craig had no idea that she was now a DJ. And since she had tried to talk and tell him whenever she was first asked about doing the job,(he showed no interest) he didn't know that her name was going to be on the billboard and if he had seen it, he didn't ask her about it. Days had passed. Kate knew that Craig had to have some idea of what was going on, but he still had not said anything to her. The base was so small, there was no way he couldn't have known. When the night came for her to D.J., Craig was so excited. He came in asking her could he help her with getting the music to the club. Kate was completely surprised. He told her that when he saw the name on the billboard he did not know that it was her. One of the soldiers had told him, his wife was working at the club also as a DJ.

Kate told Craig that she was trying to tell him but he brushed her off. (as if he didn't want to hear what she had to say) But it would be great if he would take the music down and put it in the car for her. And he did. She never asked him was he going to stop by the club or go on his happy way to do other plans. Because it seemed as if though they had been living separate lives. It was so sad, but she was enjoying her life. She was going on cruises and enjoying everything. She told Craig she was not falling for his unselfish behavior.

Her and Andrew became the best of friends. Craig told Kate he knew she was doing something because, she was never home and he knew she was not working all the time. He had the nerve to tell her if she was doing anything that she shouldn't be doing and he caught her, she would be sorry. Kate just laughs because of how ridiculous does he sound telling her something like that. Knowing that he was doing whatever he wanted to do. Being with the German women was something that he had promised her that she would never have to worry about experiencing with him. But she told Andrew that she should have known better after knowing he had been with the Japanese women. Kate continued to be a D.J. Everyone enjoyed her because she was a very outgoing person. Craig began to every now and then to come to the club and see her in action. Later Craig would always slander her about how she went from working in accounting, bar manager, bartender and now a D.J. Kate came up with an idea for the club. They should serve soul food one night out of the week. The owner thought that was a good idea for the restaurant inside the club. She got involved in that and all of the soldiers loved & enjoyed the meals because they were not used to getting a meal like that. Instead of Craig giving support and happy for her he had nothing but insults, but she did not let it stop her or affect her. Andrew was very good with supporting her and when she needed to vent, he always seemed to know what to say and what to do. When she would spend time alone with Andrew she knew it was wrong. Again she would think in her mind, "how could something feel so right, but be so wrong."(she would think about the way Craig was treating her, made this feel so right.) Kate began to travel. She went to England, Berlin, Europe and Denmark. Craig did not want to go. He kept Patrice and Nikeel. She was determined that she was not going to live oversees and not travel. She would invite Craig but he would say no, which was ok with her. She would get with the girls and they would have a great time. (no men included) In England, it was so amazing how it looked outside. Europe, Berlin and Denmark was so clean but England was very dirty on the outside. It looked like the United States but all four places were great places to visit. Kate finally took a look at what was happening in her life. She was working, spending a lot of time with Andrew and traveling with the girls. She was not spending enough time with the kids. When Craig saw that she had slowed down, he got that old cocky way that she did not care for. He told her it was about time that she decided to stay home. She quickly let him know that she wasn't doing it for him, she was doing it for Patrice and Nikeel. But she did not stop enjoying life. The landlord saw a great part of Craig actions and she did not like what she saw. She didn't like the way he would talk to Kate.

Kate would always talk to the landlord and let her know that she didn't know and understand him, she just knew she had married her husband to be forever. Patrice was 11 years old and the teacher sent a letter from school stating that when she turned 12 her school status would be changing. Patrice would have to leave on Monday and stay on a campus like the college kids for the week. She would come home on Friday afternoon. Kate knew she was not liking that. Kate asked Craig what were they going to do. Maybe it was time for them to go back to the United States. She told him they had been over there for four years and some months, they had bought nice things from over there. But Craig told her that he was not ready to go back and he was not going to put in for any orders to go back to the US. (if they did not tell him to leave he was going to stay as long as he could stay.) she told him, "fine" and that Patrice would not be 12 for another year. So she continued to work, going to see different sites, and every now and then Craig would ask her to go out with him to the German clubs. He loved to go there. Kate would always ask him why did he like to go there. He would tell her because the liquor was cheap, but she knew it was more to it than that of why he would love to go there. She knew that her marriage would never be the fairy tale she thought it would be. Everything Craig had promised her in the past was not true.

Kate had slowed down but Craig was taking advantage of her. He felt as though he should be so controlling. She never thought her marriage could be so terrible. But she loved her kids and she would do whatever it took to raise them. It was Christmas, (1988) Kate and the kids had decorated. They loved that time of the year of the year because the Americans decorated with the colorful lights and the Germans would decorate with all clear lights. The Christmas parades were very exciting. It was so much to see where they lived that they never had to take the kids out. They could stand upstairs, opening all the windows in the front and sit in the window ledges and look at the parades. Patrice and Nikeel really enjoyed it. Kate and the kids had put up the tree and had been out shopping. Craig comes home and tells her that he needed to talk to her. Kate sat down, not believing what she was hearing, it was two weeks before Christmas. Craig told her that he will be getting tickets for her and the kids to go home. Again, Kate could not believe what her ears was hearing. She asked him why was he buying tickets for them to go home. He told her because he wanted a divorce. Kate became very angry and disappointed. She asked Craig could he at least wait until the first of the year. Craig was not willing to cooperate with her at all. He had changed in so many ways. He wanted everything to go his way. He had changed to the point that there was no compromising. Kate could not talk to him anymore because it would always lead into a bad argument. Kate never saw this coming. Craig had never showed her that he would treat her so brutal and uncompassionate. She continued trying to get him to wait until the first of the year. He told her "no." She laid in bed through the night, crying her eyeballs out. Questioning herself, "how would she be able to tell the kids that they would not be sharing Christmas with him?" She was also thinking about, having to go back without him having to stop in New York. The next morning, she tried to talk to Craig again. He yells and say, "I have already told you what was going to happen, & that he was getting the tickets—case closed."

It was Saturday morning, when the kids got up, Kate had cooked breakfast. Oh how was she hating to tell the kids the news, but she knew she had to.

She knew that telling Nikeel would not be as bad because he was only six years old. But she didn't knew how Patrice would handle the news because she was eleven years old and was also daddy's girl. But again it had to be discussed because she knew that Craig was not going to change his mind in any kind of way. There would be so much to do before they could leave, how was she going to tell her job and friends. Kate just was not looking forward to none of these things to do. But she knew she had to get started packing and getting Patrice records from school. There was so much to do but Craig did not care. Everything was to be his way and what he wanted. Everything had to be done on his time. It upset Kate so much that she felt if he didn't have any more love or feelings for her, what about their kids. But she got busy and she told the kids. As for Nikeel, he just looked and not really any questions. However Patrice had many questions and Kate didn't have answers. Kate told Craig that he needed to sit the kids down and talk to them, but she was not ready for him to tell them that they would be getting a divorce. She advised him to just tell them that they were going back home because he would be getting orders later. She finally got him to come in agreement with this. Also, when calling home she would only tell their families, that her and the kids were coming home for Christmas. With every thing seeming to be in line of trying to keep the family out of what was going on. Kate still had to face her friends and coworkers on base. She knew this would be the hardest task, because everyone would have so many questions. But since Craig was not going to change his mind about them leaving she asked him could he please get the flight straight to Myrtle Beach so she would not have to stop in New York. She did not want to stop there with the kids because it is such a congested area. She went to work, hating to see anyone because her eyes were so red and puffy from crying. But she knew she had to go. Everyone was upset. They could not understand why Craig would want to do this. Kate did not want to tell anyone why this was really happening. She also knew that she had to see Andrew and tell him she would be leaving, as he had been a great friend. Although when everybody would see them together they thought they were having an affair. Andrew and Kate were never sexually active. Andrew respected Craig but he did not like how he treated her. She would often tell Andrew that if he had not been there for her she don't know what she would have done. So whenever she met with Andrew and told him she had to leave, he was very angry. Knowing that Craig was doing this within two weeks before Christmas. He felt he could have waited until the first of the year. She told Andrew she felt the same way but Craig seemed that he could not understand. But she felt as though he understood but he was just very selfish so she was going to give him his wish. It should not have made a difference how he feels about her, he should have thought about his kids. Apparently whatever he wanted to do for the holidays, it was not including his family. She told Andrew it's was his(Craig)loss and her gain. He would see those days again. She thanked him(Andrew) for being a good friend. When she knew anything Andrew was hugging her, telling her he would miss her, and he wanted her to take care of herself. Kate turning him loose to turn her head so that he would not see the tears running down her face. She left saying those same words to him. When she arrived back home she began packing as much of her and the kid's stuff that they would be able to carry. She was so glad the kids were bigger at this time to be able to fly and they would have a flight directly to Myrtle Beach. It would be so great. When it came to the day for them to leave Kate felt very emotional because, to see Patrice and Nikeel crying and asking Craig all sorts of questions, he knew not tell them a lie, so he couldn't say anything. But Kate knew if he had any heart and loved the kids, he should have felt very bad for his actions. Again, it should have not been anything about how he felt about her, he should have thought about what would he be putting

Mary K. Green

his kids through. And what kind of impact it would put on their lives. But apparently he didn't think about any of that. Kate had to do all the talking and try to make them comfortable and feel good about going home. She began telling them how excited they should be about going home to see everybody and how they would be to be able to eat some southern food. When Kate and the kids entered the plane they went to the back. It seem that was were all the party people were sitting.

The plane was very large, a 747, there were lots of seats, the plane was not full, so Kate was able to sit the kids right across from her. This way she could see them at all times. After getting them positioned and situated with the Television, coloring books and crayons, Kate could get comfortable and relax. She had a few drinks and played cards. The stewardess came around and made sure everyone was comfortable with snacks, meals and drinks. It seemed as everyone was having a ball. The kids had fell asleep. Then all of a sudden the stewardess came over the speaker phone and said, "everyone must get to their seats and get buckled in, the plane was running into a bad thunderstorm." Everyone that had a glass or was drinking an alcoholic beverage was glad to put their cups down. They could look out the windows and see the bright lightning on the wings of the plane, then the plane began to rock. They announced that the plane was running in very bad turbulence. Kate had never experienced anything like that but she knew they had to Pray. And if they didn't know how they learned very quickly. The thunderstorm was so bad, that when everyone heard the plane was finally landing in Charlotte, each one as they would get off the plane they were very glad to kiss the ground. Everyone had been so shook up that they had to get a motel room. They explained to the passengers, that because the turbulence was so bad they were going to stop in Charlotte and then after a few hours they would be going to Myrtle Beach. But no one wanted to go any further on this flight. They would rather start over the next day. And that was what everyone did. They checked in a room in Charlotte for the night. The next day they headed to Myrtle Beach. When Kate and the kids arrived into Myrtle Beach, Kate's sister (Chicken) picked them up from the airport. Because she was aware of everything that was going on and what had happened in Germany, but Kate had asked her not to tell anyone. After the kids reached Kate's mom home they were so happy to see each other because it had been about six years since they had visited. Patrice and NIkeel had grown up so much. Patrice was twelve and Nikeel was seven.

As everyone gathered together, with only three days left before Christmas, Kate went out with her sisters (Chicken and Twetty Bird) and did a few last minute shopping. It was very nice, but never letting the family really know what was going on with her and Craig. Only Chicken knowing, but she had promised that she would not say anything to anyone. Kate trying as hard as she could to adjust back to the states. As the new year approached Kate knew she would have to start thinking what she was going to do, where would she live, put the kids in school, getting a job and of course the list goes on and on as a parent. Patrice and Nikeel seemed to be adjusting well but Kate was beginning to miss being in her own place to have her privacy. So she began looking for a job, and she did not stop. Whenever she did find a job, she had two jobs that were side by side. One was at a pharmacy as a cashier and the other at a grocery store as a cashier. She was able to get the kids enrolled in school. She worked as hard as she could and tried to get as many hours as possible. Then she began saving her money, purchased her a small car, and she found a one bedroom apartment. Her and Patrice slept together in the bed and she would make Nikeel a bed on the floor. It was rough and different but it was good to be out on their own. She would take the kids out to the country as much as possible so they could get to know more about their grandparents. How glad was she that she had done this because, not even a year had passed, in 1989 her father became ill. Her father use to be in the Army, so he was rushed to the VA hospital in Charleston, South Carolina, where they had to do a scheduled surgery on his heart and he did not come out of it. He died hours afterwards on the recovery table. What a devastating time for the entire family. Her father was a great man. He would give you his last, down to the shirt off his back if he had to. Her mom was so hurt because she had lost her soul mate. Her mom and dad were very close it really took a toll on her mom. Within a year later she (Kate's mother) died. Kate and her siblings felt so very lost without neither of their parents around for them. Then within a few months later Craig called Kate and told her to give up her jobs and take Patrice and Nikeel out of school, he wanted to try their marriage again. She was so excited because after going through with losing her parents, she thought this was the greatest thing she could have heard. So she did just that. Craig was to come to Myrtle Beach and stay a few days with his family and then they would be going to Washington State. The day Craig arrived in Myrtle Beach, Kate had talked to her sister in law (Chunky Lee) she asked her to keep the kids for a few days so that when she picked Craig up from the airport they would stay in Myrtle Beach overnight and then come out in the country the next day. She was all for it. Kate was so excited, she had packed everything up for storage if needed. She felt like maybe her dream was not over. When arriving at the airport she found out the plane would be delayed from New York because they were having bad weather. They told her it would be about a two hour delay, so she went to the phone in the airport and called Chunky Lee and talked to her until she heard them announce over the intercom that the plane would be arriving from New York in 15 minutes. She got off the phone and went to the gate that Craig would be walking through. She was looking her best, she had went and had her hair done, bought a new outfit, and being so excited to see Craig because they had not seen each other in two years. The last conversation they had was that he would be glad to see her and the kids, he love them, and how they were going to make up from the time they had been apart from each other. But oh my God, what could have happened between the last phone call and the delay of his flight? It's was like he made a 360 turn around. When the plane landed, Kate was standing at the gate, everybody walking pass, and then finally Craig came. Craig walked past her, she was thinking in her mind, "like, did he not see me?" So she walked behind him, following him, and when he stopped it was at the luggage pick up area and she asked him, "Craig, Hi, did you not see me?" He looks at her and says, "yes, I seen you but right now I am trying to get my luggage." Kate is standing looking real puzzled, thinking that this is not good. After all the luggage seem to be there, the gentleman told him his luggage would be delayed until the next day. Well things started from there, Kate asked the question, what would he like to do? She told him the plans she had made. (the motel) He threw his hands up and looked at her and said, "take me to my mama house, I have changed my mind, we are not going to Washington State, I want a divorce." Kate and Craig were standing in the middle of Myrtle Beach airport and he tells her something like this. Kate remembers people looking all around because she began to just cry and cry because she could not believe what she was hearing. She told Craig where the car was, he told her "no", he would call someone to come and get him. Kate told him, "no", she wanted to drive him because she wanted to know what could of had happened from one conversation to the next few hours. He was very short with words as they rode. She asked him how could he do something so dirty. She had taken the kids out of school and she had quit her jobs. When reaching his mom's house they got out of the car, his mom came to the door, and as they embraced each other, Kate standing behind him crying her eye balls out, told him to tell his mom what he had just did at the airport. He wouldn't say anything. But when Kate opened her mouth to say something, his mom said, "I don't want to hear it." Kate became very hysterical and devastated, she knew this was her son but she had always told Kate that she was like a daughter to her. Kate felt this was the end of her life, she took her wedding rings off and threw them at Craig. She then got in the car and began to drive. She felt she didn't have anyone. Chunky Lee, she still had Patrice and Nikeel so Kate went back to the apartment where she had everything packed up, went through the boxes until she found the medicine bottles. (Tylenol pills.) She poured them by the handful in her mouth with a glass of water, but when she tried to swallow the water with the pills they would not go down. She just began to yell at the top of her lungs. Her neighbor heard her because she was so loud. She came rushing in, being in shock for what she was seeing. But Kate told her she didn't want to live, she had no parents and then Craig done what he did, she didn't have anything else to live for. Her neighbor Tina talked to her for the longest and told her she was going to call Chunky

Lee who was Craig's sister but everyone knew that Kate was very close to her. Chunky Lee came and was very upset for everything that went on. She told Kate that she was a good woman to be able to drive him out in the country because she said she would have never had did it. She would have let him get his own ride. Kate had a brother (Frogman) he lived in Raleigh, North Carolina. Chunky Lee called him and told him what was going on and she asked him to come and get Kate and she would keep Patrice and Nikeel. Kate could not think. All she wanted to do is get away from everything and everyone. She was not very excited about anything, she felt her entire life had been taken away from her. After getting to Raleigh, staying for two days, Patrice called her and she said, mama, "I heard what daddy did to you, but are you going to leave me and NIkeel here and walk away like he did?" Kate with the phone to her ear sitting, and something snapped in her mind. She told her twelve year old child, "no way, mama will be back home tomorrow." When Kate got off the phone all she could think about was her children. She called her brother (he was at work) and told him she was so thankful that he came and got her, but she had to go back. Because she had a lot to live for. She had Patrice and Nikeel and she didn't want them to think she was walking away and leaving them with someone else, even though it was their aunt. So Frogman did just that, he took her back after getting off of work. When Kate reached the kids she held them for a long time with tears running down her face. Thinking what would have really happened with them if she had lost her life for just being hurt by a man. So she began to pray telling God thank you for not letting it occur. She promised God never again would she ever let anyone get her to that stage of mind.

The next day Kate began her life all over again, she went back to her apartment to talk to the landlord about getting her old apartment back. He gave that back to her, she went back to work at her jobs, it's like everything was just waiting for her to return. And the kids went back to their school and resumed as normal. Time had passed, Craig finally called and told Kate that she would be served the divorce papers. She felt like that was going to be the next worse day of her life. But as the day approached, which was so rude of him, the date of court was her birthday, May 1993 but it turned out to be a great day for her. The judge was in favor for her. Kate got her divorce and moved on with her life taking care of her kids, who were the most importance of her life.

Chapter 5

But as Kate continues with this book, you will be reading how and who could make this possible, for anyone to want to continue to live. She started to have a big problem about dating. She felt that this one man had messed her life up totally, she never wanted to get married again, she just wanted to play the game. She dated, but never got serious. Craig had no clue how he had really hurt her. She had a wall built so high that she felt she could not trust any man that may try to come into her life.

In 1995 Kate was at work, trying to do her best job of course. She began feeling ill, and very dizzy. Since she was a manager, she had to do a lot of walking around. The clerk had went to the bathroom, a customer came into the store, and she went to the register to wait on the customer. As she turned to go back to her office, she did not remember what had happened after that. All she knew, was the paramedics was standing over her. The clerk said that when she came out of the back, there was a customer calling for help, and Kate was laying on the floor. She had fallen behind the counter, so they dialed 911, she was rushed to Grand Strand hospital in Myrtle Beach, South Carolina, Kate was hospitalized for seven days. She came out of the hospital and went back to work, back to her life routine, children, work and party every chance she got. As time progressed, she started seeing and feeling a change within her health. She knew she was beginning to gain more weight and her breathing was getting bad. She started going to the doctor and getting checked because she was thirty three years old and was feeling very tired all the time. She knew she worked two jobs, but was still trying to party also. After running test, the doctor had diagnosed her with asthma and bronchitis. She was put on thirty six pills per day. Kate would say she felt like a walking drug store. Her health kept going further and further downhill. Patrice had graduated from high school and Nikeel was in the ninth grade. The doctor told Kate she would have to stop working. After he told her that she began to cry in the doctor's office, to hear that she had to make such a drastic decision. She told the doctor that she had to work because she had one child that was in her first year of college and also a ninth grader. He told her he was sorry, but she would not be able to go back to work. Kate had no idea what she would do, because the kids had no one else but her that was providing for them. The doctor told her that he would do everything he could do to help her get onto disability. Kate was not wanting to hear any of this because she had been raised to be very independent. But she did what the doctor told her. She applied a few weeks after the doctor visit for disability. The doctor did just what he had promised and within two months she was approved.

It seemed as if her health had began to get worse, she was going to so many different doctors. Her primary doctor had put her on these thirty six pills per day. There were times when she would start to feel better, she would still try to party. But as time progressed, Kate became even more ill. She lost her voice, had to be hospitalized again, this time her immediate family had to be called in. The doctor told Kate, because she had lost her voice her wind pipe was closing she had a lung that had collapsed. He also explained to her, that it looked as though, in order for her to ever talk again, she would have to talk through a voice box for the rest of her life. Because she could not talk or when she did you could barely hear her, she pointed for a sheet of paper and a pencil and wrote down what she wanted to say. She wrote down these words, "no I don't want that, I know what I have to do." The doctor asked her if she was sure, he also told her, they would have to put a tube down her throat until she would be able to fully breathe on her own. She told him ok. He walked out of the room, Kate knew she could not get out of the bed to pray, but she laid her head back and told God this, "Lord I know I have not done right in my life time, but if you forgive me for my sins and don't let me have to talk through a voice box for the rest of my life, I will come out of the streets and live for you." Kate figured it seemed what she was doing with her life was not working. The doctor entered back in the room, he said, "Ms. Lewis, what is going on, your heart rate has turned around for the better?" Kate began to cry and pointed for the sheet of paper again. This time she wrote, "you may not know what happened, but I do." For she knew God had heard and answered her prayers. She stayed in the hospital for several weeks, but as time passed Kate was back home with her family. This time when she went home, she did not listen to her friends when they would call and wanted to go out, she would tell them "no." She knew she had to do what she had promised God. Kate began to get her life together, she started going back to church. At this time she was living in Longwood, North Carolina where her mother's brother and his wife had took her and the children in to live with them and took good care of them. There were times when Kate could not even get out of bed. But she had a praying aunt. Kate would listen to her praying day and night.

As her days were not feeling promising to her because she would feel so sick sometimes. She would be in and out of Brunswick County hospital in North Carolina very often. Until this one day, the family came in and saw that some things was not going right. They requested that she would be transferred to another hospital. Since she had a brother(Frogman) that lived in Raleigh, North Carolina, they had her transferred to Duke hospital. When Kate arrived there and was under a different doctor's care, they told the family, "this is what's killing her, those pills," he told them, that she was taking too many pills (36 per day). Kate was so happy to hear that. The doctor began gradually taking her off the medication, he narrowed it down to eight pills per day. She began feeling better, and was released to go home. Kate started feeling like God was still trying to tell her something. After returning back home to her Uncle and Aunt house, she started picking up the bible and began reading it little by little. It soon was everyday at reading of God's word. It seemed to be helping her more and more. Even though she was no longer in the clubs, like she promised God, she was still not living right, after all she had been through. Kate's cousin owned a mobile home that was vacant. He and his wife let Kate and her children move into it. She ended up meeting this man, his name was Ivan. He was this tall, thick man, and nice looking. She began to have her eyes on him and decided to give him some time. She had always told herself, because of what Craig had done to her, she was never going to marry again. It was 1996 when she had met Ivan. They started dating and she was letting him live with her and the kids. Nikeel seemed to really enjoy his company. All Kate could think about, "Ivan was the father figure that Nikeel never had in his life." As time went by, the more Kate would read the word of God, she knew that she could not continue to live that way. So Ivan asked her to marry him. Kate said, "yes" even though she had said that she was never to get married again. But Kate felt she needed someone to help take care of Nikeel financially. At this point she had gained quite a bit of weight over the years. So she started setting the date for them to get married. They knew they didn't really have the money to have a big wedding so they planned a nice reception. They went to the courthouse September 19,1997 and got married. Kate had lost over one hundred pounds so that she could get into the dress that she wanted to wear. Everything was beautiful. After getting married they decided to move back to South Carolina. (Kate's hometown). Ivan's mother lived in Florence, South Carolina. But they were living in New York for years. After Kate being married to Ivan for one year, she was cleaning their house one day and he had left his wallet home, while he was at work. There it was, on his dresser and whenever Kate picked it up, his driver's license fell out. Whenever she looked at the license it was as if his birthday was staring her straight in her face. She looked at the year he was born, it stunned her, she had to take a seat. She saw nothing but red lights going off and on in her eyes, as he had switched the numbers around of his age. At this time Kate was 36 and he had told her he was 32, when he really was only 23 yrs. old. Kate felt like a fool, how could she have missed that. She knew that some will say that age is nothing but a number. She became very angry, whenever he got home from work, it was not a good day. She began to ask questions. He told her that he was sorry but he knew if he would have told her his true age, she would not have married him. Kate told him that he was very wrong for that, she felt like she had made the worst mistake of her life. Because if he would lie about something as simple as that, what else would he lie about? Their marriage was very bad after that. Every year Ivan would have to find a new job, because he could not hold a steady job, she told him, that, after finding out his true age, she knew that he was not ready to settle down. Then after seven years of putting up with his foolishness, Kate told him that he had to leave. Both of the kids had graduated from high school, and both had started college. Nikeel was able to go all the way and get his degree, but Patrice dropped out because of a pregnancy. But as their mother, I can truly say, "God could not have given me any better children," in spite of all that we had been through. Especially a boy that could have chosen to be on the street corners at anytime doing all the wrong things, that he may have thought, that he was bigger enough to do, but he chose not to. The both of them have always respected me as their mother and we always had a great relationship. Now they are grown and have their own families. This lets me know and hopefully inspires other single mothers that maybe experiencing this same heart break, that, we as women can do it, with a man or without one if necessary. And as Kate had made a decision before, she knew she had to get up and be doing something and not get back into the same situation as how she was with the separation from Craig or when she was hurt by him. Kate would tell her family she felt so violated because if he would have told her the truth, she may be would not have been going through that. As time passed she began to read the word of God more. She found out everything she needed to know, was in the word and hands of God. Everything she had already experienced and what she was going through at the time the only way she was going to be able to survive was to turn her life completely over to God. She had to be fully committed. She had been going to church but she had not fully surrendered. Later she found out that there is a difference. A person may know God and go to church, but if they were still continuing to be of the world, they were truly not saved. But she knew she wanted more, when she thought back of what she tried to do while going through problems with Craig from the hurt he had brought to her, God stepped in and saved her with Grace and mercy from trying to take her own life. At that moment, she knew there had to be a better way or plan so that she could become fully committed. Her first change began when she fully committed herself to reading her bible more. The second change came, thru the church that she attends. They had started a morning prayer service at 6:00 am every Sunday morning, she would attend. The second change that had also come within her, when she started realizing, she was gaining strength by going to lay before the Lord, at the altar, she would talk to Jesus day and night no matter where she was. She learned that her strength had came from learning that Jesus was all she needed. Scriptures like Phillipans 4:13, I can do all things through Christ who strengthens me, Psalm 23—The Lord is my shepherd I shall not want, Psalm 37:3-4 Trust in the Lord and do good, so shalt thou dwell in the land and verily thou shall be fed. (4) Delight thyself also in the Lord and he shall give thee the desires of thine heart. Proverbs 3: 5-6, Trust in the Lord with all thine heart and lean not unto thine own understanding. (6) In all thine ways acknowledge him and he shall direct thy paths. There were many others, but these stayed within her mind at all times. Kate started going back to church on a regularly, attending the church that she started going to with her parents from childhood. Now that she was building her relationship with God and was under the leadership of a new pastor, she rededicated her life back to God and the church. After all these changes had been made within, she felt brand new. There would be no more playing church, because when God dealt with her, she heard a soft voice say, "be real." Kate knew she had to be obedient, especially for what all the things God had brought her through. Often there were times that sickness would come upon Kate during church service, she felt as though God would let it happen in church around many people to let them see what prayer could do. Yes, prayer can change things. It is the key that opens the door. But as some may read Kate's book, they may be saying to themselves, "if she was sick when she was in the world and still had health issues, even after her change, what was the need of making a change in her life?" Well, let Kate explain :When a person is living as being of the world and not in the word, if they die, as living that life, they are on the road/path to hell. The bible says, "we must be born again." And one can find meaning of this Romans 10:9, "That if thou shalt confess with thy mouth the Lord Jesus, and shalt believe in thine heart that God has raised him from the dead, he shall be saved." During the times thru all of her sickness and even when it seemed like there were no ending to her storms, she still continued and pushed to get closer to God. For she had already experienced what the world had to offer her. Hebrews 13:5, "I will never leave thee nor forsake thee." also Matthew, 16:26 told her, "For what is a man profited, if he shall gain the world, and lose his own soul? Or what shall a man give in exchange for his soul?" This helped Kate come to realize that when she was of the world, she didn't understand how to deal with any storms, sickness, or death. But as she kept reading God's word, she found the answer. "If God be for us, who can be against us?" Romans 8 :31. As you continue reading Kate's book, she will tell you about her last terminal illness, that she often still continue to fight the battle, but she knows that she could only have been saved by God.

Chapter 6

After Kate had been through the many years of battling sickness, on April 13, 2010, she was at home, when she stood up, as she began to try to walk, her steps were very slow. She noticed that she was dragging her left leg. She did not have any idea what was going on. Her sickness before was related to respiratory problems (breathing problems). She had suffered obesity for a while, therefore she knew this was not the same. She was home alone on that day, so she called 911. When the paramedics arrived, they began to check her vitals, afterwards they informed her that they would be taking her to Grand Strand hospital, located in Myrtle Beach. After arriving there, they began running test, when they received the test results, they came in and said they could not find anything wrong. Kate and her family became very disturbed upon hearing this news. Because, she was dragging her left leg, they felt as though, that was not normal. Later another nurse came in and told her they were going to be sending her home. Kate's daughter, Patrice and her sister, Tweety Bird, became very outraged. They told the nurse to call the doctor down to the room who was sending her home, because they wanted to talk to him. They waited and waited, he never came. Kate began to speak, she asked them to call Nikeel, her son. When reaching Nikeel, she took the phone and began to explain what was going on. He told her she could not go home. For her to hold on until he got off of work. She told him ok. Whenever Nikeel got off work, he came to the hospital and told her he would be taking her to MUSC, a hospital in Charleston, South Carolina. By the time they arrived to the hospital(MUSC) Kate's temperature was 103*. MUSC did not hesitate, they took her in right away, asking many questions. They began running more test, their test results showed she had a staph infection. The doctors explained that it is in the family of MRSA(Kate didn't know what that meant). They explained, it was a very bad infection and if she had of went home, she may not have lived to see the next morning. He told the family that they would be admitting her to the hospital, and would do all they could. Kate laid there for 23 days with temperatures ranging from 103*—104* degrees. Some of those days, not even realizing anyone was there to visit her. Everyone stuck by her during this time, coming to visit as often as possible. Her kidneys began to shut down, but as everyone prayed, things began to look up for Kate. Her fever began to break, temperature was lower, and her kidneys began to work normal again. Oh how glad was everyone to hear of the great news.

Because the doctor had already told the family that she might would have to start taking dialysis. But God already had a plan. He made sure she did not have to experience that. After two days of Kate showing improvement of health, the hospital decided to move her to a nursing home—rehabilitation center. When arriving at the nursing home/rehab center, Kate realized that the only part of her body that she could move, was her head. She then became very frightened, as there was none of her family around at the time. Instantly Kate began to yell and scream as loud as she could, until someone would come into her room. The nurses came running to her room, they began telling her that she was still in Charleston, but had been moved to a nursing home—rehabilitation center. The nurse explained to her that, the reason that she couldn't move any parts of her body was, because all of her muscles had went to sleep. She had lost all her feelings in her entire body. Kate couldn't even give herself a drink of water. She tried to move her legs, they would not move, they told her she could not walk. Kate was not understanding and of this what was happening so she just began to cry.

They told her the doctor at MUSC had explained everything to her prior to them moving her, but she could not remember any of that. They told her that her family was very aware of what was going on and they were on the way. Kate still was not understanding, she kept asking them, "was she paralyzed?" They tried very hard to assure her that she was not paralyzed, it was only that all her muscles had went to sleep. Finally, the doctor and her family came in. (She felt really like the whole world was falling down on her.) The doctor told Kate the reason she was placed in that facility where she was, because she needed medical attention around the clock and she would have to regain feeling of her body and learn to walk again. Whenever she would try and sit up she would fall backwards. She was really disturbed with the fact of she had to wear depends. (diaper) As tears fell from Kate's eyes, the Dr. told her, she was a lucky woman, and that most people did not live through what she had experienced. Or this type of infection. Again, Kate had questions. She wanted to know where did this type infection come from, or how did she get it? The doctor explained, that a person can catch it from being in the hospital, bathrooms, or anywhere. This was a type of infection that could be contagious at times, therefore, it was possible that she could have gotten it just from being around people. Kate looked at him, still in tears, and said, "I'm not lucky, I am Blessed." He told her and the family, he did have any idea of how long she would have to stay there, she had a long way to go for getting well. They would have to keep her on a antibiotic intravenously(IV) for eight weeks to get rid of the infection. She would have therapy five days a week. But the family could come up and visit her at anytime. Kate told her family that she did not expect them to come very often because it was about a two and a half hour drive. Her brother Frogman, who lived in Raleigh, North Carolina it would probably be about a four and half hour drive for him. The family told Kate that she didn't have to worry about them and their driving, because they would be there for her just like they were at MUSC or Myrtle Beach. (Kate did not remember all of the times they visited her at MUSC.) Well it was time for everyone to leave, Kate tried to keep a straight face and not cry. After everyone had left the room, she really did breakdown and cry. Because she felt so helpless and she began thinking of all the horrible things that she had heard about the staff that worked at nursing homes. That some were very mean and don't take good care of patients. But as she was sobbing, she began to think what she really needed to do. That she had to pray and believe God was going to take care of her while she was there, because she could not go home. Everyone was working and she had to have someone to take care of her. She was going to trust God, that she would not be there for a long time, it was only temporary.

Day after day as Kate laid there helpless, struggling with not being able to walk and no use of her hands. It seem as though that was the hardest time and test that she had to overcome. Some of the staff at the facility were not nice, but Kate held on, she prayed and as she journeyed, she became stronger. The therapists she had were great people. When they came in and saw Kate's condition they began doing all they could do for her to try and help her walk again. Weeks had passed, Kate began getting strength in her hands. When doing so, the therapist ordered for her some long straws. Kate was getting very excited, she would be able to get a drink of water and would not have to call anyone. Kate stayed at the nursing home/rehab center for eight months. By this time, she was moving her hands, arms, legs, and could turn over and sit up again. Family and friends were there for her. When they visited, someone would always take the time and feed her. During Kate's stay as she began to get stronger, she would tell the nurses or nurses aids that were so mean and seemed as if they hated their job, how independent she was before she became sick. She would tell them that they maybe up today but they didn't know what they may endure in life before they leave this world. Or they should take in consideration if it was one of their close loved one's, that she was sure they would want someone to treat them with respect. After Kate started expressing her feelings, they thought twice how they would act.

To anyone who maybe reading Kate's book, always remember, no one wants to put their love one's in such a place, but when it comes to a situation that you can not help or do not have control of, you may not have choices, but to put them there. She also wants to share with you, if it comes to a crossroad in life and any of you do have to put your loved one in a nursing home, don't forget about them, make sure you visit them, because that means so much. And when any facility find out that you are visited on a regularly basis like Kate family and friends did, they told Kate at the facility she was at, they had no choice but to take care of her because they could not believe that someone was there two and three times a week.

They had to keep her clean. When Kate would go by some of the rooms, they would tell her, that some of the people in the facility, did not have any visitors, since they had been put there. Please know that it helps the person to keep holding on and it is very lonely when they don't see or hear from anyone.

Finally they told Kate that she could go home, after being there for eight months. When she arrived home, she had been blessed with an addition on her home. They had built a wheelchair ramp. Although she was confined to a hospital bed, she could feed herself, but still could not walk. As she laid there day after day she had to keep her mind focused on God, because it was becoming depressing. Family and friends took very good care of her. Days would pass by and sometimes it seemed as the walls were closing in on her. After being home about three months, it seem it was getting to be too much. So Kate decided that she wanted to be put back in the center. But instead she ended up back into Grand Strand hospital. This time her stay was about 10 days and then the doctors decided to send her back for more therapy. This time she was sent to a different nursing home-rehabilitation center. The facility was located in Georgetown, South Carolina. Kate was glad God had answered her prayer, because she saw it was getting to be too much for her family to take care of her, because they had to go to work.

When Kate arrived at this facility, she found out that her therapist that was assigned to her was going to push her very hard. But Kate realized to get where she needed to be, it was going to take hard work. Kate put her mind on Jesus, and every time it seemed as if she could not take it or did not feel like going for therapy, she would begin thinking about, who could move her feet so she could walk again, because Luke 1:37, "told her For with God nothing shall be impossible" and Kate believed that. She knew that it did not look like what it may have seemed if she trust in God and have faith of mustard seed. (which is very small)It was the last of January, 2011, Kate was there with a great spiritual leader, she was hard, but very encouraging. Kate would have to have her bath and breakfast by 7:30am every morning, then she would be taken to the therapy room, where there she was to use the exercise equipment. She fell in love with the bicycle. She would sit and move her legs hours and hours sometime, unless someone else would need to use it. Also, through this ordeal, she was realizing, that there was beginning to be a tremendous weight loss. So by talking to a dietician she let her know that she wanted to continue the same diet when she go back home. She was very happy for the weight lost, because her breathing was getting better. She kept working out and praying to walk again. And around the first week of March, Kate awakening, as a usual morning routine, before her therapist came. When her therapist came that morning she told Kate, that she would be letting her try to take steps from the room instead of them pushing her down to the therapist room in a wheel chair. She wanted her to try to take some steps. When Kate sat up on the side of the bed, after they help with putting on her tennis shoes, she stood on the side of the bed with a walker in front of her. As she began to move the walker, she felt her feet moving, Kate had taken a few steps. Suddenly she stopped and looked around and told her therapist that, "she had to excuse her for a few minutes. She had to give God a praise, because only he could do something so great." Kate was very excited, because she held on even when she wanted to give up. Everyday that Kate stayed at the facility she was walking better and better. After about three weeks there, they told her that she could go home at the end of the month. And Kate did. When reaching home again she, still had to go through therapy at home. A month later after being home, she took her first journey back to church, were she missed so much.

The Sunday that she was going to church, "Oh" what a reunion, her therapist (Teresa) & mother, Kate's children, grandchildren, her husband, sister, and nieces and nephews and of course friends. It was a blessing to see them all, her pastor and church family they could not always go to visit her at the center, as often as they would have like to but, they continued to pray for her and trusted God to bring her back to them. Kate is still struggling to gain her full independence. After a few more months and being home again, she is still having to visit doctors, but as days come and go, she is trying to keep her eyes on the Lord. Because she does not take the storm or issues she may have faced in the past or still maybe facing, as a punishment. She believes that people has to face things in order to help someone else. So when things occur in your life whether you are trying to live right or not. Saved or not saved, we are not excluded from anything because we have to look at what Jesus did for us and what he took. Don't get mad, know that God made us and your life was already planned before you were born.

But Kate wanted to share with you her life story, to let you know, that it took for her to get to a point of her life, where she was sick and tired of the way she was living. she wanted to make a change. And when a person start feeling and thinking that they will want to confess their sins. Then you will learn to pray and trust God because he made us and he is the only one to know what we can be, so don't ever settle for where you are at. Because as we keep living in this world that God created, but man is making it be rough roads to travel. If we have experienced many things in life and still here everyday, God still waking us up, we should want to turn our lives around. Because the world don't mean us no good. We might as well surrender our life over to God. Is this saying to us if we make a change that everyday will be good, all the time, "no", but this will help us to make better decisions. It will teach us how to live down here better, teaching us we have a choice, we can go to Heaven or Hell. If it seems we are living in hell here on earth everyday, it is because we are allowing man/flesh to make it that way. Ask yourself this question, if reading or being told Kate's story, "what is required of me to go to heaven?"

If I am living an unstable life and I don't change I could be on my way to hell. I would want to give up some things to make it to heaven. So Kate encourages each and everyone of you to make the turn around in your life, because it is never too late. Even as you are still reading, before Kate does the closing of her book, she wants you to know, that she is still on going to therapy, but God is still showing favor in her life. She is now having pool therapy, which is really helping. Muscles are really waking up and she has the heart and courage to keep going, as God continues to do what he has promised. She is keeping her faith and walking in her healing, even though she has not gained her full independence back as of yet. But, because of her belief in God, she never stopped giving God her praise.

For he is working all things out for her. She is getting to go to church more, she does telephone ministry, and she talks to God and lets him know that when he does give her full independence, she will be obedient and go out and tell the world of his great work. (What God has done, no man on can do) As for her and Ivan, it is in God's hands what the outcome will be. As for the future, Kate cannot predict, but some of the things that she does know, that are planned for the future, is, her daughter Patrice has informed her that she is engaged.(Kate is so happy for her) She has planned a wedding date for June 8,2013. This gives Kate more stability and encouragement to fight harder for independence. Because after Patrice's marriage, Kate will have to begin taking care of herself. As she has learned through, Philippians 4:13, "I can do all things through Christ who strengthens me." Kate has given her daughter all her blessings for her upcoming marriage. She continues to pray & in hopes that she never in life have to go through what she had to go through and her marriage will be all that she is looking for. Kate would also like to share with you that when she look in the mirror every morning and everyday, at 54 yrs. old, she thanks God every day that she does not look like what she has been through. (others often tell her that also) At this point of her life, she does not take anything for granted as she knows that it is the hands of God that has been laid upon her. She is going to and will endure all things until the end. No matter what may come her way.

I am hoping and praying, as the author of this book, that you have enjoyed Kate's life story. In chapter 7, she is leaving you with a few scriptures, to encourage you, "no matter what your life living maybe, Jesus is the way, you can't go wrong."

Chapter 7

In this life in general today, at some point everyone is going to experience something, it may come with hurt, where there is pain behind it. Or it maybe only a test of your faith, to see if you will be obedient. A lot of us say that we know God, but the question is, "do you believe and trust?" Always remember the three P's of your life. (Purpose, Plan, and Pay Off) When you think of these "P's" and still of the world-the definition only defines itself for each.

Purpose: The reason for which something exists or has been done.

Plan: A drawing made to scale of a new building or project

Pay Off: The money to be used to be to pay workers. Now let me explain these 3 valuable "P's from the Spiritual side. These "P's" are granted from God, as he already has the answers.

Purpose: Everyone has purpose on their lives (Test)

Plan: Your life was already planned out before you were born(No door shall close, without another opening)

Pay Off: To make the change in our lives, and have love for Christ (We will see Jesus-come on in my child)

Scripture to uphold these "P's":

Jeremiah 1:5-"Before I formed thee in the belly, I knew thee, and before thee comest out of the womb, I sanctified thee, and I ordained thee, a prophet unto the nations.

6-"Then said I, Ah, Lord God! Behold, I cannot speak, for I am a child.

7-"But the Lord said unto me, say not, I am a child for thou shalt go to all that I shall send thee, and whatsoever I command thee, thou shalt speak.

If we confess our sins and turn from our wicked ways, most of all do what thus says the Lord. That's our "Pay Off" when we go to Heaven. Everybody is born in sin, but the bible will teach you, how we should live by his commandments, because as sure as we are born, we will die. We have a choice of how we want our pay off. Good or bad, if you learn to read his word, get in a spiritual ram(church), and under good leadership, we will find out that whenever we close our eyes there is no return, but God holds the gates. There is nothing in our lives that we may experience, that is so bad that one can't be saved. There no problems so big that God can not solve.

Matthew 6:33-"Seek ye first the kingdom of God, and his righteousness, and all these things shall be added upon you."

Romans 10:9-"That if thou shalt confess with thy mouth the Lord Jesus and shall believe in thine heart that God hath raised him from the dead thou shall be saved." When you are saved, you have to learn that you can not serve both, the devil and the master. But oh my God when you can let your flesh die, you will learn to love, even when someone has done wrong by you. Continue to pray for them and know that whatever issue or storm occurring in your life, give it to Jesus, and he will fight your battle. (the battle is not ours)

Romans 8:31-"What shall we then say to these things? If God be for us, who cab be against us?"

32-"He that spared out his own son, but delivered him up for us all, how shall he not with him also freely give us all things?"

33-"Who shall lay anything to the charge of God elect? It is God that justifieth."

34-"Who is he that condemneth? It is Christ that died, yea rather that is risen again, who is even at the right hand of God, who also maketh Intercession for us."

35-"Who shall separate us from the Love of Christ? Shall tribulation, or distress, or persecution, or famine, or nakedness, or peril, or sword?

36-"As it is written, For Thy sake we are killed all the day long, we are accounted as sheep for the slaughter."

37-"Nay, In all these things we are more than conquerors through him that loved us."

38-"For I am persuaded that neither death, nor life, nor angels, nor principalities, nor powers, nor things present, nor things to come."

39-"Nor height, nor depth, nor any other creature, shall be able to separate us from the Love of God which is in Christ Jesus our Lord."

Kate is now closing her book, with hopes that whoever has purchased a copy, it has touched them, in some type of way. Please continue to pray for her that she may continue to be blessed and she will be doing the same for you. Remembering the Foot prints in the sand.

May God Bless all of You!

Mary K. Green

"Footprints in the sand"

One night a man had a dream. He dreamed he was walking along the beach with the Lord. Across the sky flashed scenes from his life for each scene, he noticed two sets of footprints in the sand one belonged to him, and the other to the Lord

When the last scene of his life flashed before him he looked back at the footprints in the sand he noticed that many times along the path of his life there was only one set of footprints he also noticed that it happened at the very lowest and saddest times of his life.

This really bothered him and he questioned the Lord about it

"Lord, you said that once I decided to follow you, you'd walk with me all the way. But I have noticed that during the most troublesome times in my life, there is only one set of footprints. I don't understand why when I needed you the most, you would leave me."

The Lord replied, "My precious, precious child, I love you and I would never leave you. During your times of trial & suffering, when you see only one set of footprints, it was then that I carried you."

About the Author

Mary K. Green is a woman of God. She inspires people with the provisions of Christ. She is very considerate and mindful of her actions which reflect the kind of person she has become as a minister.